# Of Life And Godliness

the Journey
to Christian Spiritual Growth and Maturity,
or How to Obtain Everything God Has
Provided for Our Life and Godliness Through
Knowing God and Hearing God's Voice

# Of Life And Godliness

the Journey
to Christian Spiritual Growth and Maturity,
or How to Obtain Everything God Has
Provided for Our Life and Godliness Through
Knowing God and Hearing God's Voice

By

Mike W. Ferry

Edited by

Patty Ferry

Foreword by

Dennis See

Pursuit Publishers

PO Box 1893

Redmond, OR  97756

Pursuit Publishers
PO Box 1893
Redmond, OR  97756

http://www.pursuitpublishers.com

ISBN: 978-1-937682-26-2

Library of Congress Control Number: 2011917023
Library of Congress subject headings:
Spiritual life--Christianity.
Christian life--Study and teaching.
Christian life.
Spirituality.
God (Christianity)--Knowableness.

# DEDICATION

This book is dedicated to the one person who first asked me if God had told me to write a book. She is the best gift that God ever gave me, next to my salvation. She is my love, best friend, and my wife of over 30 years, Patty.

Patty, just like Jesus, you have always believed in me. I love you!

# CONTENTS

# FOREWORD

I have known Mike for years and have watched him grow in the things of the Kingdom of God and his relationship with the Lord Jesus Christ, and it has been a wild and awesome journey. Mike has lived and walked out the things he is talking about in this book. I cannot think of anyone better to listen to with the wisdom and insight he shares here.

The different areas of love, faith, and relationship with the Lord that he writes about will transform your life. It will give you insight and help you on your journey as a Christian, if you will listen to, and walk in, the wisdom he shares. Its truths will strengthen you and keep you from many pitfalls throughout your life. It will help you build a strong, deep, and lasting relationship with the Lord. It will help you become unmovable and unshakable in your faith, and it will cause you to mature.

I highly recommend repeatedly reading this book until you extract every insight from its pages. I found myself getting excited again about my relationship with the Lord and the possibilities He has for me as I grow to know His precious Holy Spirit.

I have walked with the Lord since April 2, 1976, and I believe this book would also make an awesome study for any believer, whether you are just new in the Kingdom or a seasoned Christian who has walked with the Lord for fifty years.

I pray for God's blessing on every page and that revelation knowledge in this book will be imparted to all who read it.

Thank you, Mike, for your obedience to write this book that I know will help many believers on their journey of "life and godliness."

Dennis See
Founder and Director, The Altar Int'l House of Prayer
Meadville, Pennsylvania
August 11, 2011

# PREFACE

As I was saying goodnight to the Lord one evening in March, 2011, He said to me, "Are you ready to write your book?" I replied, "If You think I'm ready, I am. What is it about?" He said, "Of life and godliness, the journey." I drifted off to sleep with that title branded into my memory. I awoke the next morning to His voice giving me instruction on how to begin the book. For several months, He continued to download the information to put into the book.

What you have in your hands is the deposit given to me to share from God's heart. Enjoy the experience.

God bless you, Mike W. Ferry

# Acknowledgments

I acknowledge and express my thanks to my lovely wife, Patty, who not only encouraged me during the writing, but also spent countless hours editing and designing the manuscript of this book. She also took the cover photograph and my photograph. This book never would have been finished or published without her help.

I am also grateful to Dennis See, who wrote such a wonderful foreword for the book. He has been a constant friend and confidant, and a source of encouragement in my life, in both the difficult and the overcoming times of my life.

To Tom and Nicole, my dear friends, for standing behind me and being my rear-guard, and encouraging me and giving me a stream of great ideas for marketing this book.

To Marcus and Hollis, also dear friends, for always being there, ready to help; for opening their home to us when we needed a place to live; for always believing in our call to pastor; and for always being ready for an evening of fellowship.

To the pastors I have had over the course of my life that helped forge me into the man of God I am now, including Jimmie Ray Cantrell, Mike Prato, Larry Black, John Kowalczyk, Bruce Ladebu, and Randy DeMain.

To my mother, for challenging me to bring clarification to several parts of this book. I love you, Mom.

To Dyan Roth, for using my wife's photograph to design such a beautiful cover.

To my intercessors and congregation, for praying me through the writing of this book.

Finally, to God the Father, Son, and Holy Spirit, without whom not one word of this book would have been written, and without whom I would not have my existence.

# INTRODUCTION

Have you ever worried about your life?

What does tomorrow hold for us? Next week, next month, or next year?

The cares of this world weigh heavily on many hearts today. When we accept Jesus Christ as our Lord and Savior, we do not need to worry about our lives any longer. 1 Corinthians 6:19–20 says we were bought with a price and we are no longer ours.

This choice to become a Christian begins our journey into God's purposes and plans for our individual lives. It also opens the way into His Kingdom and places us under His divine protection and provision.

In this book, I share truths from God's Word, which will encourage your heart to be all God desires you to be in your daily life. God's promise from 2 Peter 1:3 is true, and will transform your life!

# CHAPTER 1

# SETTING THE STAGE

Growing up in the church, I have noticed in the lives of many Christians the driving desire or obsession to obtain. As I endeavored to begin this book, I felt that this was the starting point to talk about life, as well as godliness, in a Christian's life. Do we have all the ingredients for a satisfying, godly life? It may sound as if we do not, if we listen to what others are saying in daily conversations. I have found that statements like, "If I had," "If I could only," "If I just," are all based from an attitude of lack. According to 2 Peter 1:3, we have everything pertaining to life and godliness through our knowledge of Him who called us. As you enjoy this book, I pray God will reveal the true depth of the revelation of what Peter is saying to us about lack.

## WHERE ARE YOU SITTING?

If you find yourself making statements like those I have described, they are indicators of a root of misinformation or a deeper illness of unbelief. Have you ever prayed, "Lord, I need Your grace," "mercy," "strength," or so forth? Those are prayers from a place of lack. Where are you sitting in a prayer like that? Those prayers do not originate from the position of sitting with Christ in the heavens.

"But God, who is rich in mercy, because of His great love with which He loved us, even when we were dead in trespasses, made us alive together with Christ (by grace you have been saved), and raised us up together, and *made us sit together in the heavenly places in Christ Jesus*" (Ephesians 2:4–6). God *made us* sit in heavenly places in Christ Jesus. This place of authority and power, as well as agreement, allows us to observe from God's point of view. As Christ is at the Father's right hand and we sit with Him, we have the authority to pray in agreement with Christ as He intercedes on our behalf. Prayers from the lap of the Lord sound like, "Thank you, Lord, for Your grace," "mercy," "strength," and so on.

We serve an awesome God who sent His son to die in our place for our sins and that son, Jesus, promises to return. Until Jesus returns, we are to live out an ambassador's life here on earth, spreading the Good News of the kingdom.

## SATISFACTION NOT GUARANTEED!

Feelings of missing out also play a part in the drive to obtain. I label those feelings as envy. Let us examine a classic example of envy. In Genesis 3, we see this trait first revealed in humanity:

Now the serpent was more cunning than any beast of the field which the LORD God had made. And he said to the woman, "Has God indeed said, 'You shall not eat of every tree of the garden'?" And the woman said to the serpent, "We may eat the fruit of the trees of the garden; but of the fruit of the tree which is in the midst of the garden, God has said, 'You shall not eat it, nor shall you touch it, lest you die.'" Then the serpent said to the woman, "You will not surely die. For God knows that in the day you eat of it your eyes will be opened, and you will be like God, knowing good and evil." So when the woman saw that the tree was good for food, that it was pleasant to the eyes, and a tree desirable to make one wise, she took of its fruit and ate. She also gave to her husband with her, and he ate. (vv. 1–6)

This same story line continues to repeat itself today. The rationalization of the fruit being good for food, pleasing to the eye, and a provider of wisdom, set in motion the fall of humanity.

The perception of not knowing enough or not having enough permeates the American dream. The old adage of "he who dies with the most toys wins" can be found everywhere in the last twenty some years. Feelings have changed from "keeping up with the Jones" to "let's go into debt to fulfill our wants." Look at the predicament we have created for ourselves through envy and by living this unsustainable standard. This very self-centered style of selfishness has gone out of control! "Satisfaction guaranteed" is not a promise in this life, apart from God, and even then, satisfaction comes from God's definition, not ours. "The fear of the LORD leads to life, and he who has it will abide in satisfaction; he will not be visited with evil" (Proverbs 19:23).

## LIVE THE DREAM

One of the inspirations God gave to me was to *live the dream God dreamed for me.* My God dreams big. I do not need all the stuff that can clutter my life to have my dreams fulfilled. Just by examining His creation, you will see all the diversity He placed there, from the micro to the macro. Everything God dreams happens. We have a personal God who is interested in all we do. The day-to-day is not mundane to God. His plans and purposes are within every day of our lives if we look for them. "Your eyes saw my substance, being yet unformed. And in Your book they all were written, the days fashioned for me, when as yet there were none of them" (Psalm 139:16). God has a specific part or dream for each of us to live out. Do you believe that about yourself? Do you believe that you can live the dream God dreamed for you? Do you believe you can live a life of full satisfaction?

If you have accepted Jesus Christ as Lord, then this scripture applies to you. "Not that I have already attained, or am already perfected; but I press on, that I may lay hold of that for which Christ Jesus has also laid hold of me" (Philippians 3:12). Think about that statement for a moment. There before us lays a journey, "line upon line, precept upon precept" (Isaiah 28:10), leading to a final destination. Christ Jesus set His eyes on you and determined that you were an incredible investment. He purchased you with His own blood and started preparing a wondrous life for you. Knowing our weaknesses, the Holy Spirit began an internal remodeling that will ultimately form us into the image of Christ Jesus. "Being confident of this very thing, that He who has begun a good work in you will complete it until the day of Jesus Christ" (Philippians 1:6). Now you and I have something to be confident about!

Within our journey, God predetermined special moments and appointments in our lives just to bless you and me. This is what God's dream looks like. Each one of these moments empowers us to experience blessings. He leaves them as presents for us to discover along the way. These blessings come in many forms. My personal desire within my life is to "lay hold of that for which Christ Jesus has also laid hold of me" (Philippians 3:12), which is His dream. My desire for you as you read this book is to see through Christ's eyes what He has for you to "lay hold of." With God, you can live the dream God dreamed for you!

## WE ARE HIS WORKMANSHIP

We have the special blessing of being handpicked by God. With this knowledge, there is an even greater responsibility, and ability, to fulfill our potential. "For we are His workmanship, created in Christ Jesus for good works, which God prepared beforehand that we should walk in them" (Ephesians 2:10). What an incredible scripture about us!

God's fingerprints are all over our lives. Not only are all our days fashioned by God but also He even went so far as to prepare beforehand great exploits for us to do. We do not want to miss even one of God's daily gifts for us. We have the ability and responsibility to answer His call to do those good works.

If you want to know what those works are, you just need to listen for His voice. He says of us, "My sheep hear My voice, and I know them, and they follow Me" (John 10:27). Knowing His voice is one of the first steps to a fulfilling life. God's voice of direction can also be a comforting companion in our daily walk. We are not to take lightly the call of God to fulfill those exploits on our life. "For the gifts and the calling of God are irrevocable" (Romans 11:29).

Paul, in Ephesians, has this to say to us as well. "I, therefore, the prisoner of the Lord, beseech you to walk worthy of the calling with which you were called" (Ephesians 4:1). We are called to greatness, not mediocrity! God does not create junk. When He created the world, Genesis 1:31 states that He saw that it was good. That creation includes you and me. God has a stake in us. No one has been an accident or overlooked by God. God desires to have a one-on-one connection with all humanity.

## It's About Relationship

As you can see, I am not talking about religion, but relationship. Religion causes us to reject the seed of revelation and leaves us holding the empty shell of the structure. With the seed of truth gone, there is no promise of the new growth. See if I am telling the truth. Go out, plant the husk from an ear of corn, and watch what grows. Now take just one fertile kernel, plant it, and see the great potential of continued harvests you reap.

This same principal holds true in our lives—relationships create life. A relationship with God is like any other that requires a continued commitment. Religion is the empty husk from the corn, a lot of activity that looks great on the outside and very little life on the inside. If you find that statement offensive, I leave this scripture with you. "I press toward the goal for the prize of the upward call of God in Christ Jesus. Therefore let us, as many as are mature, have this mind; and if in anything you think otherwise, God will reveal even this to you" (Philippians 3:14–15). In other words, our individual godly calling may cause misunderstandings or even conflict between brothers. So let us agree at this point and *from this point forward*—if we disagree, God will reveal the truth to us. This understanding should be the tie that binds us together in love with our fellow Christians, as stated in Colossians 3:14.

## The Abundant Life

As we have a personal relationship with God, He reveals to us specific secrets that we need to understand to fulfill the call upon our lives. "Whoever has been born of God does not sin, for His seed remains in him; and he cannot sin, because he has been born of God" (1 John 3:9). The word *seed* here is the Greek word σπέρμα, which is transliterated "sperma"[1]. Does that word look familiar? The living *seed* that remains in us carries the dynamic creative power of the Almighty God! Its creative force is a constant in our spiritual growth and life. Without it, we are nothing more than empty vessels or wells without water.

Life without the seed is *not* living the abundant life that Jesus promises when He says, "The thief does not come except to steal, and to kill, and to destroy. I have come that they may have life, and that they may have it more abundantly" (John 10:10). Do you have the seed of God within you? I ask you, are you living or just surviving?

## Our Journey Is With God

"Blessed is the man whose strength is in You, whose heart is set on pilgrimage. As they pass through the Valley of Baca, they make it a spring; the rain also covers it with pools. They go from strength to strength; each one appears before God in Zion" (Psalm 84:5–7). This sounds like living to me! Put yourself in this verse and see what God has intended for you.

We draw our strength from God and God alone, and we are on a journey. "He restores my soul; He leads me in the paths of righteousness For His name's sake" (Psalm 23:3). We are going where He leads. We do not need to struggle along, fumbling for the correct direction to go.

Look closely at what verse 5 of Psalm 84 says: "Blessed is the *man*" (singular). In verse 6 it says, "As *they* pass..."—that is the man and God together. Wow! We set our heart on this pilgrimage and we go out with God by our side. What a reassuring promise we have of not being alone against the world and its trials.

Next, they arrive at the Valley of Baca or Valley of Weeping. Here, God's power transforms the place of weeping into the descriptive picture of an oasis with pools, which are produced by *rain.* This sounds like God raining down blessing on us.

Finally, we see God and this individual going from strength to strength all the way to Zion. I picture myself walking triumphantly hand in hand with God as we take on all challengers in this life, as He leads me in victory.

## KNOW GOD INTIMATELY

It requires intimacy to obtain this type of relationship. Let us look at the story of the woman at the well, found in John 4.

Jesus tells her all about herself, yet had never met her before. She runs into the city and tells her friends all about Jesus and many believe in Him on her testimony alone. Still others come out to inquire of Christ themselves and ask Him to stay on for several days. This group would not accept secondhand knowledge to convince them of who Christ was, but listen to what they later said: "Then they said to the woman, 'Now we believe, not because of what you said, for we ourselves have heard Him and we know that this is indeed the Christ, the Savior of the world'" (John 4:42).

Everyone fits in one of these categories—either firsthand or secondhand knowledge. I want firsthand knowledge of someone, so I can stand next to him or her without a doubt in my mind. I want to hear for myself and know someone's heart, like those who came to listen to Jesus.

Listen to Peter as he proclaims to us, "But you are a chosen generation, a royal priesthood, a holy nation, His own special people, that you may proclaim the praises of Him who called you out of darkness into His marvelous light" (1 Peter 2:9).

King David in the Psalms states, "He also brought me up out of a horrible pit, out of the miry clay, and set my feet upon a rock, and established my steps" (Psalm 40:2). Do you feel the desire of God for you? You are chosen, special, called, and established by Him. Do you want to know Him firsthand or secondhand? Above all, *we must know God intimately.*

## IT IS NOT THROUGH THE LAW

The reading of this book may stir many to begin a regimen of activities based on rules found in the laws of the Old Testament. That is *not* God's or my desire for the reader. I will address the law in a later chapter but first let me say, fulfilling the law is Christ's duty alone, not ours. Let me quickly share these:

Do not think that I came to destroy the Law or the Prophets. I did not come to destroy but to fulfill. (Matthew 5:17)

There is therefore now no condemnation to those who are in Christ Jesus, who do not walk according to the flesh, but according to the Spirit. For the law of the Spirit of life in Christ Jesus has made me free from the law of sin and death. For what the law could not do in that it was weak through the flesh, God did by sending His own Son in the likeness of sinful flesh, on account of sin: He condemned sin in the flesh, that the righteous requirement of the law might be fulfilled in us who do not walk according to the flesh but according to the Spirit. (Romans 8:1–4)

Thank you, Lord Jesus! This is the sure foundation of a Christian's life.

## REVELATION, SALVATION, SANCTIFICATION

Let us take a moment and see what else our marvelous Savior has done. "Husbands, love your wives, just as Christ also loved the church and gave Himself for her, that He might sanctify and cleanse her with the washing of water by the word, that He might present her to Himself a glorious church, not having spot or wrinkle or any such thing, but that she should be holy and without blemish" (Ephesians 5:25–27). Here we see Christ using His Word to sanctify and cleanse, so that He may present us to Himself as a holy, glorious church without fault.

As to the workings of this "washing by the word" in my own life, I have found this formula tends to be true. *Revelation* brings *salvation,* which brings *sanctification.* This formula plays out something like this.

Revelation is God *revealing* by His Word, either written or spoken, that I have an issue, which separates me from Him. "For all have sinned and fall short of the glory of God" (Romans 3:23).

My response is then to confess it. "If we confess our sins, He is faithful and just to forgive us our sins and to cleanse us from all unrighteousness" (1 John 1:9). Here the salvation comes through the cleansing—God saves and delivers me from my old ways of living.

Finally, the sanctification is received with the washing away of the sin. "And such were some of you. But you were washed, but you were sanctified, but you were justified in the name of the Lord Jesus and by the Spirit of our God" (1 Corinthians 6:11).

Again, we see it as a work of Christ or His name. Can you envision Jesus looking at you and seeing all the defilement upon you? His response is not repulsive but a genuine desire to touch you and wipe away the grime to allow everyone to see what beauty lies beneath. His gentle touch removes the smallest fleck left behind, then presses out the wrinkles, and erases every spot. He speaks words of comfort and love with each touch. You can see the love in His eyes for you and hear it in His voice.

## JESUS' BRIDE

I would like to share a vision I had many years ago of a wedding. I saw a small church nestled in a wood; I could smell the deep aromas of the moist earth and woodland. Inside the church a wedding was about to take place.

At the front stood the groom and the facilitator who would be conducting the ceremony. The music started and all arose for the bridal march. There at the back of the church stood a young woman.

She wore a tattered, stained dress with bare feet covered in filth. Her hair was matted; her hands were rough and calloused, with dirt under each nail. Her veil was tipped to one side and torn, and her teeth were broken and rotting.

The groom turned and awaited His bride. As the bride took her first steps forward, a gasp went up from the congregation. The bride continued down the aisle and all began to murmur. The bride had been oblivious of her appearance and hesitated half way down the aisle.

The people all stared and pointed in disbelief at the bride, which caught the attention of the groom. Suddenly He realized what was occurring and swiftly rushed to her side. As He reached her, His touch instantly transformed her into the beautiful bride He had already been viewing through His eyes. Together they proceeded to the front.

I believe this simple vision represents what happens to us as we come to Christ. We are oblivious of the filth and situation of our appearance. However, Christ quickly rushes to our aid to show all how He perceives us.

I hope that I have eased some of your concerns about your own salvation. I also hope that I have challenged you to venture into a closer walk with God. May you experience His touch and encouragement in your life and watch closely for all the daily blessings from God to you. May you also know how He feels toward you!

I will close this chapter with this marvelous promise. "The Spirit Himself bears witness with our spirit that we are children of God, and if children, then heirs—heirs of God and joint heirs with Christ, if indeed we suffer with Him, that we may also be glorified together" (Romans 8:16–17).

# CHAPTER 2

# MY RESPONSIBILITY

What an amazing potential we have as God's children! Because we are God's children and coinheritors of God's Kingdom with Christ, according to Romans 8:17, what expectations are there for us to fulfill? In this new relationship, we will grow and experience many changes in our lives. As a Christian, what can we expect? How can we prepare for what lies ahead? The Bible holds all the information we need to build an understanding of God's ways and how to prepare for the future. The work of the Holy Spirit in our lives holds an important influence for direction and change. Together the Word and the Spirit are an unbeatable pair who can transform our lives in powerful ways.

## THE TIME TO COME

Fearsome times are coming on the earth, and as Christians, we need to be prepared. Life can get out of control quickly. We must incorporate into our lives the ability to apply God's Word quickly in all situations. In the following passage from Luke, Jesus gives us two building blocks of truth for our life.

> So they asked Him, saying, "Teacher, but when will these things be? And what sign will there be when these things are about to take place?" And He said: "Take heed that you not be deceived. For many will come in My name, saying, 'I am He,' and, 'The time has drawn near.' Therefore do not go after them. But when you hear of wars and commotions, do not be terrified; for these things must come to pass first, but the end will not come immediately."
>
> Then He said to them, "Nation will rise against nation, and kingdom against kingdom. And there will be great earthquakes in various places, and famines and pestilences; and there will be fearful sights and great signs from heaven. But before all these things, they will lay their hands on you and persecute you, delivering you up to the synagogues and prisons. You will be brought before kings and rulers for My name's sake. But it will turn out for you as an occasion for testimony.
>
> Therefore settle it in your hearts not to meditate beforehand on what you will answer; for I will give you a mouth and wisdom which all your adversaries will not be able to contradict or resist. You will be betrayed even by parents and brothers, relatives and friends; and they will put some of you to death. And you will be hated by all for My name's sake. But not a hair of your head shall be lost. By your patience possess your souls. (Luke 21:7–19)

There are two ideas I want to propose to you from the above scripture. The first is clear and easily understood. He exhorts us to be not terrified and to settle it in our hearts. We are to trust the Holy Spirit to provide for our defense in the presence of our adversaries. The second is the use of our patience to possess our souls. The Greek word found here for patience is ὑπομονή (or hypomonē), which can be translated as *endure, enduring, patience, patient, patiently*.[2] We will discuss this further in a few moments.

## NO FEAR!

God is challenging us to be bold in difficult times. Fear does not belong in the life of a Christian. Just look at the events Jesus named: wars, earthquakes, famines, pestilence, "fearful sights," and "great signs from heaven." It sounds as if the entire world is in upheaval, both physically and spiritually. In addition, Christ describes Christians' closest family and friends betraying them, resulting in a death sentence. This may sound like a good time to be in fear, but not according to Jesus. Christ's word of encouragement is to endure or be patient amid these events, and to possess our souls.

As tragedies, adversities, and other challenges occur in life, we need to stay focused on God and His benefits. This is a good place to discuss Romans 8:28: "And we know that all things work together for good to those who love God, to those who are the called according to His purpose." God controls it all! He turns every event to His purpose and plan. Even when we cannot see His plan, He works things out for our benefit, because we love Him and are "called according to His purpose." Amongst all the chaos and confusion in life, God's Word is true.

All the difficulties try our hearts and our devotion to Him. I know from my own experience that there are many trying times in our lives and we often may feel we face them alone, but that is a misconception. "Let your conduct be without covetousness; be content with such things as you have. For He Himself has said, 'I will never leave you nor forsake you.' So we may boldly say: 'The LORD is my helper; I will not fear. What can man do to me?'" (Hebrews 13:5–6). Jesus said He would never leave us alone— what an awesome promise! Jesus never breaks a promise, so in difficult times we must not only stand on the promise but also proclaim the promise!

Hold on to His Word and promises and you will not fear or fall, because perfect love casts out fear. "There is no fear in love; but perfect love casts out fear, because fear involves torment. But he who fears has not been made perfect in love" (1 John 4:18). In all our lives, trials come and go, but God always remains. I have found that searching for Jesus in the tragedy always provided the strength to overcome.

## POSSESS YOUR SOUL

Let us discuss possessing our soul. It is time for some more Greek studies. First, let us look at the word *possess* in the Strong's dictionary. It is the Greek word κτάομαι (ktaomai), also translated as *get, got, gotten, obtain, obtaining, possess, possession, provide, providence, provision, or purchase.*[3] The capturing or the ownership of a given item sums up the meaning of the word "possess." I chose these two characterizations because of the weight both carry. If I *capture* someone, I can arrest them, seize them, apprehended them[4], and wrestle them into submission. If I have *ownership* of a given item, I have lordship, dominion, possession, or authority over its use and conduct.[5]

Now let us turn our attention to the soul itself. It is the Greek word ψυχή, which reads "psychē," which can be translated as:

doubt (be in; make to), doubtful, doubting, heart, heartily, life, living, lifetime, life-giving, and soul.[6] For some time, the definition of the soul has been described as the mind, will, and emotions of an individual. With this in mind, we can intertwine the three thoughts of capturing, ownership, and soul to get the implied interpretation we need. Luke 21:19 could now read like this: "By your [enduring trust and faith in God's protection and provision], [arrest, seize, and wrestle into submission by taking lordship, dominion, possession, or authority] over your [mind, will, and emotions and their conduct]." What a mouthful. I wanted to expand on this statement by using these descriptive words to paint the full picture of how we are to respond. Savor the statement for a moment before you read on.

## VICTORY

Jesus said, "These things I have spoken to you, that in Me you may have peace. In the world you will have tribulation; but be of good cheer, I have overcome the world" (John 16:33). Jesus was preparing His disciples for the difficult times that lie before them. What better word of encouragement do we, His current disciples, need to hear?

In the darkest times of my life, I found that as I questioned God on important points, His response has been, "Do you trust Me?" It did not seem to matter how trivial or desperate the question was, the answer was the same. God's statement may seem like a shocking response, which ignores my direct question, but is actually a corrective word meant to keep my eyes on Jesus. Jesus is not only a one-time victor, but He continuously leads us in victory.

"But thanks *be* to God, who gives us the victory through our Lord Jesus Christ" (1 Corinthians 15:57). We can find victory in life, but only by God's definition. In human understanding, when did a crucifixion ever describe victory? Only once. The cross of Christ for the lost is the perfect victory. Death on the cross at that moment looked like defeat, but the results of His death brought victory. Hallelujah!

How much more can the tests in our lives look like defeat in the moment, but instead are treasured victories. Psalm 66:10 reads, "For you O God have tested us; You have refined us as silver is refined." The testing of our hearts brings forth the true treasure in us. Tests come in every shape and size. I believe each test is a proving ground to our faith and the redemptive work of God in our lives. The products of these tests are just as diverse as the test itself, but our faith increases as well.

## Treasures of Wisdom and Knowledge

Listen to what the apostle Paul has to say about treasures in Colossians 2. "For I want you to know what a great conflict I have for you and those in Laodicea, and for as many as have not seen my face in the flesh, that their hearts may be encouraged, being knit together in love, and attaining to all riches of the full assurance of understanding, to the knowledge of the mystery of God, both of the Father and of Christ, in whom are hidden all the treasures of wisdom and knowledge" (vv. 1–3). Hidden in the Father and Christ are treasures of wisdom and knowledge. When a challenge presents itself, we need both wisdom and knowledge to respond correctly, and the faith to persevere.

Stamina is a necessary ingredient in a Christian's life. It takes determination to keep pressing forward, when all those around you say to give up. The negativity of others can be taxing. Psalms 68:9–11 says, "You O God, sent a plentiful rain, whereby You confirmed Your inheritance, when it was weary. Your congregation dwelt in it; You O God, provided from Your goodness for the poor. The Lord gave the word; great was the company of those who proclaimed it." God affirms us as His inheritance as He rains down blessings and provision in view of the unbelieving around us. The rain is also to encourage us and bolster our determination to press on, especially when we are weary. We are to live daily in the blessed rain of His presence. We qualify as poor when we are weak, so He provides His goodness to us, making us strong and rich. Being in the rain confirms us as His, and we in turn have the privilege of proclaiming *we are His!*

God's desire is that we would know Him in all His attributes and ways, drawing forth His wisdom and His knowledge. Knowing Him may sound difficult but He is reaching out for us, just as much as or more than we are reaching for Him. The purpose of our drawing wisdom and knowledge from the Father, as well as Christ, is for the expressed purpose described in Matthew. "Then He said to them, 'Therefore every scribe instructed concerning the kingdom of heaven is like a householder who brings out of his treasure things new and old'" (Matthew 13:52).

A similar scripture in Proverbs reads, "There is desirable treasure, and oil in the dwelling of the wise, but a foolish man squanders it" (Proverbs 21:20). God has blessed each of us with His wisdom. The illustration here is that to hoard or waste the desirable old and new treasure and oil, from God's purpose is foolish. The momentum of Heaven depends on such wisdom; it is not just for us as individuals—we must share it with others. The "foolish man squanders" wisdom by hoarding it away for himself— he does not share it with others.

It is fulfilling when God uses us to share His Kingdom principals with others. The gift of watching a brother or sister in Christ light up as the Spirit reveals truth to their innermost being blesses both God's and my heart. We must share what God has entrusted us with others.

## TRUST IN THE LORD

"Wisdom and knowledge will be the stability of your times, and the strength of salvation; the fear of the LORD is His treasure" (Isaiah 33:6). When difficult times come, what will you hold on to for stability? "Some trust in chariots, and some in horses; but we will remember the name of the LORD our God" (Psalm 20:7). His name is our stability and He is our rock of salvation. God's name will be the strength of your salvation. "The name of the LORD is a strong tower; the righteous run to it and are safe" (Proverbs 18:10). His name is the name above all other names, according to Philippians 2:9.

When we were children and something challenged us, where did we go? I hope that it was to our father. I find it reassuring that we never outgrow our heavenly Father's side. You are not a coward when you run to Him. Real men (and women) know when to run to the Father.

Difficult times call for wise actions. God is building His church and providing for the coming challenges that will face all humanity. With God, we will stand and face these difficult times head on. Let this scripture be an encouragement to you:

Therefore, my beloved, as you have always obeyed, not as in my presence only, but now much more in my absence, work out your own salvation with fear and trembling; for it is God who works in you both to will and to do for His good pleasure. Do all things without complaining and disputing, that you may become blameless and harmless, children of God without fault in the midst of a crooked and perverse generation, among whom you shine as lights in the world. (Philippians 2:12–15)

His children will exhibit godly boldness in the last days in amazing exploits of the kingdom. The church will shine as never before. Get ready, church, for an astounding outpouring of God's glory and power.

## YOU ARE BEING WATCHED

We must do all we can to walk worthy of the call. 2 Corinthians puts it this way—"You are our epistle written in our hearts, known and read by all men; clearly you are an epistle of Christ, ministered by us, written not with ink but by the Spirit of the living God, not on tablets of stone but on tablets of flesh, that is, of the heart" (vv. 2–3). Whether you like it or not, those around you ("a crooked and perverse generation" (Philippians 2:15)) are constantly watching you and how you act as a Christian. Our transformation is God's handiwork. He enables us to desire to do His will, and fulfill His desires for us. We must be obedient and not *complain or dispute* during our training. In so doing we will become the blameless and harmless children of God.

The most difficult part to explain to those observing us is the transformation we must go through as we grow. We will make mistakes, but God will deliver and change us. He explained this process to me with the idea I previously discussed—revelation brings salvation, which gives sanctification.

## GOD MADE US TO BE HOLY

Therefore gird up the loins of your mind, be sober, and rest your hope fully upon the grace that is to be brought to you at the revelation of Jesus Christ; as obedient children, not conforming yourselves to the former lusts, as in your ignorance; but as He who called you is holy, you also be holy in all your conduct, because it is written, *"Be holy, for I am holy."* (1 Peter 1:13–16)

I believe God proclaims this statement over us similarly to His proclamations in Genesis of "Let there be…," which created the heavens and the earth. As we face our sins and confess them to God, He proclaims over us, *"Be holy for I am holy."* The creative power of God speaking this over us can transform those weak areas in our lives. The *seed of God,* described in 1 John 3:9, in us because we are born of Him, will enable us to walk sinless before Him.

We will stumble throughout our walk, but we have this promise found in Psalms: "The steps of a good man are ordered by the LORD, and He delights in his way. Though he fall, he shall not be utterly cast down; for the LORD upholds him with His hand" (Psalm 37:23–24).

Here it is described differently, "For a righteous man may fall seven times and rise again, but the wicked shall fall by calamity" (Proverbs 24:16). To know that God delights in my way and that He will uphold me gives me the courage to face every new day with its challenges. Knowing without a doubt that God is watching out for me gives me hope when I fall to temptation.

When we do fall and the Spirit convicts us, we may feel as Isaiah did:

So I said: "Woe is me, for I am undone! Because I am a man of unclean lips, and I dwell in the midst of a people of unclean lips; for my eyes have seen the King, the LORD of hosts." Then one of the seraphim flew to me, having in his hand a live coal which he had taken with the tongs from the altar. And he touched my mouth with it, and said: "Behold, this has touched your lips; your iniquity is taken away, and your sin purged." Also I heard the voice of the Lord, saying: "Whom shall I send, and who will go for Us?" Then I said, "Here am I! Send me." (Isaiah 6:5–8)

To be in the presence of God and know you are sinful is a sobering thought. The confession of Isaiah initiated the seraphim's response with the fiery coal to purge his sin and take away his iniquity. The same exchange occurs each time we confess our sins. If our sins are forgiven each time we repent, then doesn't that mean we are without sin? Can we truly walk a sinless life? I believe so. If we are being made "into the image of [Christ]" (Romans 8:29), who was sinless, then I believe it is possible.

## YOU HAVE A DESTINY

With this invitation to "be sent" that we read in Isaiah, how we see ourselves is very important to how we walk out our destiny. Isaiah says, "Here am I and the children whom the LORD has given me! We are for signs and wonders in Israel from the LORD of hosts, who dwells in Mount Zion" (Isaiah 8:18). The writer boldly announces that he and his children are for *"signs and wonders in Israel."* Knowing God had sent him with a mission, enabled him to fulfill his destiny. Do you know this about yourself? God has sent you with a purpose, and your life has meaning. Your life has a divine destiny. Hear it again—you have a purpose and destiny!

## BE BOLD AND VICTORIOUS

As Christians, we need to embrace fully what I term *the heart of the lion tamer*. "Be sober, be vigilant; because your adversary the devil walks about like a roaring lion, seeking whom he may devour" (1 Peter 5:8). Because the devil is *like* a roaring lion, we need to be *like* the lion tamer. Boldness is needed to walk out God's purpose for us. I do not know about you, but I am not in the mood to be devoured!

Yes, we are in a battle. Let me briefly describe that battle. Because of the enemy's sin, God cast him out of Heaven. He was conquered, degraded, and put to shame! He knows he could not wage another attack on the Father and His armies with any hope of victory, so what did he decide? "I may not be able to beat God, but I can go after His children!" The devil turned his deep-seated malevolent hatred on humanity.

Praise the Lord for His provision for the final destruction of *our* foe! Hear the words spoken to Joshua and take them as your own. "Have I not commanded you? Be strong and of good courage; do not be afraid, nor be dismayed, for the LORD your God is with you wherever you go" (Joshua 1:9). Together we are, and will continue to be, victorious in Christ Jesus.

What value do you place on yourself? The preciousness of Christ's blood is an indicator of the value God places on you. We must also recognize that the Father places all of heaven's resources at our disposal to establish His will on the earth. The truth we see here should propel us forward in faith to see His will done on earth as it is in heaven.

I have heard it quoted, "Never give up, never surrender[7]." It takes determination to face the challenges of life. I base my determination on the Word of God. In Isaiah 54, I find I have a heritage. "'No weapon formed against you shall prosper, and every tongue which rises against you in judgment You shall condemn. This is the heritage of the servants of the LORD, and their righteousness is from Me,' says the LORD" (Isaiah 54:17).

I am not standing alone. God fills my mouth, if I allow Him, with the authoritative words of condemnation to those rising against me. God says my righteousness is from Him. This place of authority and victory is the position to start a battle from.

## HEIRS OF THE KINGDOM

One of the simplest ways to please our heavenly Father is to receive the kingdom from His hand. Remember Luke 12:32: "Do not fear, little flock, for it is your Father's good pleasure to give you the kingdom." Just think about that statement for a moment. The Father gets much joy giving the kingdom to His children.

As children, we must learn Kingdom dynamics—how God's kingdom works around us, in us, and through us. This training comes about under the guidance of the Holy Spirit, as revealed in John 14:26: "But the Helper, the Holy Spirit, whom the Father will send in My name, He will teach you all things, and bring to your remembrance all things that I said to you." Simply said, if God's Word is in you, the Holy Spirit will bring particular scriptures to memory to fit each situation as it arises. I encourage you to study the workings of the Spirit on your own.

## ON THE KING'S BUSINESS

Because we are heirs to a kingdom, we should expect God to send us out to perform kingdom business, just as an ambassador of a country can complete business for that country. Luke 10:1–24 shows us what it is like, when God sends us out to represent His kingdom, to do the business of His kingdom:

After these things the Lord appointed seventy others also, and sent them two by two before His face into every city and place where He Himself was about to go. Then He said to them, "The harvest truly is great, but the laborers are few; therefore pray the Lord of the harvest to send out laborers into His harvest. Go your way; behold, I send you out as lambs among wolves. Carry neither money bag, knapsack, nor sandals; and greet no one along the road. But whatever house you enter, first say, 'Peace to this house.' And if a son of peace is there, your peace will rest on it; if not, it will return to you. And remain in the same house, eating and drinking such things as they give, for the laborer is worthy of his wages. Do not go from house to house.

"Whatever city you enter, and they receive you, eat such things as are set before you. And heal the sick there, and say to them, 'The kingdom of God has come near to you.' But whatever city you enter, and they do not receive you, go out into its streets and say, 'The very dust of your city which clings to us we wipe off against you. Nevertheless know this, that the kingdom of God has come near you.' But I say to you that it will be more tolerable in that Day for Sodom than for that city.

"Woe to you, Chorazin! Woe to you, Bethsaida! For if the mighty works which were done in you had been done in Tyre and Sidon, they would have repented long ago, sitting in sackcloth and ashes. But it will be more tolerable for Tyre and Sidon at the judgment than for you. And you, Capernaum, who are exalted to heaven, will be brought down to Hades. He who hears you hears Me, he who rejects you rejects Me, and he who rejects Me rejects Him who sent Me."

Then the seventy returned with joy, saying, "Lord, even the demons are subject to us in Your name." And He said to them, "I saw Satan fall like lightning from heaven. Behold, I give you the authority to trample on serpents and scorpions, and over all the power of the enemy, and nothing shall by any means hurt you. Nevertheless do not rejoice in this, that the spirits are subject to you, but rather rejoice because your names are written in heaven."

In that hour Jesus rejoiced in the Spirit and said, "I thank You, Father, Lord of heaven and earth, that You have hidden these things from the wise and prudent and revealed them to babes. Even so, Father, for so it seemed good in Your sight. All things have been delivered to Me by My Father, and no one knows who the Son is except the Father, and who the Father is except the Son, and the one to whom the Son wills to reveal Him."

Then He turned to His disciples and said privately, "Blessed are the eyes which see the things you see; for I tell you that many prophets and kings have desired to see what you see, and have not seen it, and to hear what you hear, and have not heard it." (Luke 10:1–24)

Several powerful truths are hidden in this scripture passage. I want to touch on a couple.

First, Christ was sending them to cities where He Himself would later visit to complete the works they had started. It will embolden our faith to realize that God sends us on *divine encounters* in our lives, and then follows up to bring completion to them.

Second, I love how Jesus describes them as "lambs among wolves," then tells them not to take provisions with them. The strongest statement that shakes me is found in verse 16: "He who hears you hears Me, he who rejects you rejects Me, and he who rejects Me rejects Him who sent Me." This is saying that if those I am sent to, reject me as God's messenger, I should not take it personally, because they are actually rejecting God and His son.

Finally, I wish for you to see Jesus' response to these events. He rejoiced in the Spirit or "pneuma," the Greek name for the Holy Spirit. As I do the work of the kingdom, He responds the same way! The Father, Son, and Holy Spirit rejoice when the kingdom advances through us. The Father has pleasure as He gives us the kingdom.

I do not want to overlook a small reference found in verse 19: "Behold, I give you the authority to trample on serpents and scorpions, and over all the power of the enemy, and nothing shall by any means hurt you." Jesus gave them that authority when He sent them, but He did not point it out until they had returned and were amazed that "even the demons are subject to us in Your name." He always equips us before He sends us out—whatever we need to fulfill our "mission" will be there for us to use, though we may not realize we have it until we need it.

It is simple to walk out our kingdom purpose on the earth, which is found in a face-to-face relationship with God. In Isaiah 30, we find a clear description of this: "Your ears shall hear a word behind you, saying, 'This is the way, walk in it,' whenever you turn to the right hand or whenever you turn to the left" (v. 21). When God sends us, we have His directive. We carry kingdom purpose and kingdom momentum. As we release that kingdom purpose, God establishes His will on the earth.

The miracles that accompanied the disciples confirmed to the people that the messengers were telling the truth about God. The kingdom of God was at hand. As these men walked forth in kingdom power and authority, they changed the earth forever, just as when we do the same.

Let me close this chapter with the reciting of Isaiah 60:1–3: "Arise, shine; for your light has come! And the glory of the LORD is risen upon you. For behold, the darkness shall cover the earth, and deep darkness the people; but the LORD will arise over you, and His glory will be seen upon you. The Gentiles shall come to your light, and kings to the brightness of your rising." God's promises are always true, so you can know that this would happen for you.

# CHAPTER 3

# THE LAW IS WEAK

In this chapter, I want to focus on the Law of Moses and its purpose, and where we can find strength to be the light of the world. In short, the Law of Moses was to give instruction on relationship with God and others. The Law was never intended to be the "Do's and Don'ts" of life. I believe that the Law's primary purpose was to reveal humanity's sin and the inability to reach God through the works of the flesh (man's attempt to reach God by his own devices) by following the rules and regulations in the Law.

## THE LAW SHOWS OUR SHORTCOMINGS

First, we will examine Romans 7, and then Galatians 3, to understand further these statements.

What shall we say then? Is the law sin? Certainly not! On the contrary, I would not have known sin except through the law. For I would not have known covetousness unless the law had said, "You shall not covet." But sin, taking opportunity by the commandment, produced in me all manner of evil desire. For apart from the law sin was dead. I was alive once without the law, but when the commandment came, sin revived and I died. And the commandment, which was to bring life, I found to bring death. For sin, taking occasion by the commandment, deceived me, and by it killed me. Therefore the law is holy, and the commandment holy and just and good.

Has then what is good become death to me? Certainly not! But sin, that it might appear sin, was producing death in me through what is good, so that sin through the commandment might become exceedingly sinful. For we know that the law is spiritual, but I am carnal, sold under sin. For what I am doing, I do not understand. For what I will to do, that I do not practice; but what I hate, that I do. If, then, I do what I will not to do, I agree with the law that it is good. But now, it is no longer I who do it, but sin that dwells in me. For I know that in me (that is, in my flesh) nothing good dwells; for to will is present with me, but how to perform what is good I do not find. For the good that I will to do, I do not do; but the evil I will not to do, that I practice. Now if I do what I will not to do, it is no longer I who do it, but sin that dwells in me. I find then a law, that evil is present with me, the one who wills to do good. For I delight in the law of God according to the inward man. But I see another law in my members, warring against the law of my mind, and bringing me into captivity to the law of sin which is in my members. O wretched man that I am! Who will deliver me from this body of death? I thank God—through Jesus Christ our Lord! So then, with the mind I myself serve the law of God, but with the flesh the law of sin. (Romans 7:7–25)

Is the law then against the promises of God? Certainly not! For if there had been a law given which could have given life, truly righteousness would have been by the law. But the Scripture has confined all under sin, that the promise by faith in Jesus Christ might be given to those who believe. But before faith came, we were kept under guard by the law, kept for the faith which would afterward be revealed. Therefore the law was our tutor to bring us to Christ, that we might be justified by faith. But after faith has come, we are no longer under a tutor. (Galatians 3:21–25)

These two passages bring to light the singular idea that the Law was to allow humanity to see its shortcomings about God's holiness. In other words, we cannot meet God's standards. Galatians 3:24 adds personality to the Law when the Apostle Paul describes it as, "a tutor bringing us to Christ to be justified." Having then been justified, the need for the tutor was no longer required because faith has come.

## CHRIST FULFILLED THE LAW

You may be wondering how I can say the Law is no longer valid. Paul, in Romans 10:4, says, "Christ is the end of the Law for righteousness to everyone who believes." Once we come to Christ, we go to another level of guardianship. We no longer need the

Law and its work is finished. We are free in Christ, and faith in His ability, with the Spirit, to finish the good work in us, is now leading our lives.

Scripture has more to say about the Law for us today:

For the law of the Spirit of life in Christ Jesus has made me free from the law of sin and death. For what the law could not do in that it was weak through the flesh, God did by sending His own Son in the likeness of sinful flesh, on account of sin: He condemned sin in the flesh, that the righteous requirement of the law might be fulfilled in us who do not walk according to the flesh but according to the Spirit." (Romans 8:2–4)

Let us compare "the law of the Spirit of life in Christ Jesus" and "the law of sin and death." The law of gravity is always at work on the earth, but because of the law of lift, we can fly above the ground when we are in a plane or glider. Likewise, when we are living under the control of the Spirit of life in Christ Jesus, we soar over the law of sin and death and all its drudgeries. Christ is the only answer, period. Christ has set us free from the Law, because the Law was made "weak through the flesh."

## Do Not Think About That!

Let me give you an example of what I am saying. If I tell you *not* to think about a warm piece of Marion berry pie with vanilla ice cream on the side, what happens? You envision the piping hot pie, nicely browned on top, the aroma it releases as you cut yourself a modest piece, the Marion berry filling oozing from the edges of the fluffy crust, the creamy vanilla ice cream, with flecks of real vanilla bean, melting and creating puddles along the edges of the plate. Now wipe the drool from your chin and see how difficult it is to control the flesh. You may be saying, "That just wasn't fair!" However, I hope you got the point. Paul said in Romans 7:8, "But sin, taking opportunity by the commandment, produced in me all manner of evil desire."

Now that we are free from the Law, how do we proceed without falling into lawlessness? The only way is through Christ's sacrifice, and the Spirit's daily guidance. "But now we have been delivered from the law, having died to what we were held by, so that we should serve in the newness of the Spirit and not in the oldness of the letter" (Romans 7:6).

The Spirit of God becomes our tutor as we embark on the path of this new life. "But if you are led by the Spirit, you are not under the law" (Galatians 5:18). In these verses, we see that the Holy Spirit will be with us. We are to be "led by the Spirit" (Matthew 4:1), "serve in the newness of the Spirit" (Romans 7:6), and to "walk in the Spirit" (Romans 8:1–4). We need to learn to trust the Spirit to lead us in our lives always.

I will let you in on a secret. However many laws or rules you restrict yourself with, you will not achieve Christ-likeness. The only thing you will achieve is bogging yourself down in self-righteous religion and finally suffocation under the continuing weight of guilt.

Let us go back to my example of the pie and ice cream. Following this type of thinking, I would have to start by clearing my mind of any pictures of the pie and ice cream. To do that, I fix my eyes on something else. If I could do that, I would have to remind me never under any circumstances to think about the pie and ice cream. To make sure I never forgot this, I would need a reminder of what I was not to think of. When guilt built up, I would need to examine the reason for the guilty feelings, which would cause me to think about the original pie and ice cream. Can you see how quickly this way of thinking leads back to the pie and ice cream?

## THE ANSWER IS IN CHRIST

We can never war against our flesh with an action of the flesh. We can never place enough laws on us to gain the victory. Look at what Jesus said to the Jews in John 5:3—"You search the Scriptures, for in them you think you have eternal life; and these are they which testify of Me" (John 5:39). The formula for eternal life is not found in the scriptures alone, but is found in the *Living Word of God,* Jesus Christ.

The Jews diligently searched the scriptures and only found a superficial understanding of what it required to receive eternal life. They thought they understood and could fulfill the requirements to receive eternal life apart from Jesus. Jesus told them the scriptures testified about Him, but they could not see the truth standing right in front of them. How very sad! What they did find was that religion blinds the eyes of those who follow it and separates them from freedom in Christ. A life based in a day-to-day relationship with Jesus is the key.

I want to share something, which may clarify what happens in a relationship with the Lord. 1 Corinthians 2:11 says, "For what man knows the things of a man except the spirit of the man which is in him? Even so no one knows the things of God except the Spirit of God." You know deep within what is true about you. The same is true about the Spirit of God—He knows all there is to know about God. "But God has revealed them to us through His Spirit. For the Spirit searches all things, yes, the deep things of God" (1 Corinthians 2:10). Because of the Spirit's knowledge, He can reveal every secret about God, and about us. I have learned from the Holy Spirit how God uses *our* spirit.

These verses are about the things God has prepared for us. Proverbs 20:27 says, "The spirit of a man is the lamp of the LORD, searching all the inner depths of his heart." The Lord uses our spirit to illuminate the dark innermost regions of our hearts and inspect them. Think about it—have you ever felt the conviction of the Spirit as He revealed your deepest thoughts, the sudden prick of what many call our conscience, that sudden feeling of being "found out?" The Lord shines His light and reveals those sinful, unregenerate things about us, that are in us.

Let us take a moment and look at Hebrews 4:

For the word of God is living and powerful, and sharper than any two-edged sword, piercing even to the division of soul and spirit, and of joints and marrow, and is a discerner of the thoughts and intents of the heart. And there is no *creature* hidden from His sight, but all things are naked and open to the eyes of Him to whom we must give account. (vv. 11–13)

The Greek word for creature is κτίσις, (ktisis), and it is translated as "build," "builder," "building," "create," "creation," "creator," "creature," and "ordinance."[8] Not only is God inspecting our hearts but also He is dissecting every thought and intention to see whether it comes from anything but Him. If there are any things not of Him, He will find them, and we will give an account of why they are in us.

Those are the actions of a loving God. If you believe those are the actions of an overbearing God, then perhaps you should re-evaluate those feelings with the Holy Spirit. You may have separated yourself from the freedom Christ purchased for you, and you are living under the deception of the enemy concerning how you view God the Father.

## THE APOSTLE PAUL STRUGGLED, TOO

With this understanding, let us review Romans 7:7–25. In verse 8, Paul is describing how sin had produced all manner of evil desires in him. "But sin, taking opportunity by the commandment, produced in me all manner of evil desire. For apart from the law sin was dead." In verses 15–17, we find Paul's sobering picture of the struggle within himself. "For what I am doing, I do not understand. For what I will to do, that I do not practice; but what I hate, that I do. If, then, I do what I will not to do, I agree with the law that it is good. But now, it is no longer I who do it, but sin that dwells in me."

Paul is telling us how he wants to do what is right, but sin keeps him from doing it, and makes him unable to respond properly before God. This is troubling to him as he writes, "I do not understand." I have felt like this at times, and these verses were the only place I found hope. I would stumble, fall, and come weeping before the Lord saying, "It's me again, I fell over the same problem. I just don't understand why!" So the war continued. Sin, the driving force, or the "creature" of Hebrews 4, opposes all the good desires to please God.

Romans 7:21–25 provides a clear picture of what I am describing:

I find then a law, that evil is present with me, the one who wills to do good. For I delight in the law of God according to the inward man. But I see another law in my members, warring against the law of my mind, and bringing me into captivity to the law of sin which is in my members. O wretched man that I am! Who will deliver me from this body of death? I thank God—through Jesus Christ our Lord! So then, with the mind I myself serve the law of God, but with the flesh the law of sin.

Finally, Paul says in verse 24, "O wretched man that I am! Who will deliver me from this body of death?" The answer is, "Jesus Christ the Lord."

## PUT THE SIN TO DEATH!

Colossians 3:5 addresses the "war among the members," as Paul describes it, where he tells us to: "therefore put to death your members which are on the earth: fornication, uncleanness, passion, evil desire, and covetousness, which is idolatry." How do we put them to death? By using the truth I described earlier from Proverbs 20:27 and Hebrews 4:13—let the Lord shine His light into your heart and repent from the evil desires which rule and reign there. God began this good work in you and me. Never forget we are being conformed into the image of His son. Romans 8:29 gives us that promise, and we are complete in Him according to Colossians 2:10.

Considering what we have covered here, I want to close this chapter with these verses:

Therefore, my beloved, as you have always obeyed, not as in my presence only, but now much more in my absence, work out your own salvation with fear and trembling; for it is God who works in you both to will and to do for His good pleasure. Do all things without complaining and disputing, that you may become blameless and harmless, children of God without fault in the midst of a crooked and perverse generation, among whom you shine as lights in the world, holding fast the word of life, so that I may rejoice in the day of Christ that I have not run in vain or labored in vain. (Philippians 2:12–16)

Picture how the Lord uses your spirit as His lamp to point out faults in you. In His love, He directs the sword of the Spirit to pierce the heart of the problem and free you from its grasp. Together, you put it to death. The "fear and trembling" are from the sobering revelation of all that He finds in your soul and His fierceness in dealing with it. His desire is for you to do all for His good pleasure. As He places His lamplight on particular sins, do not deny or complain they are not yours, but confess those sins to Him. This is the transformation of who you are into a blameless child of God. Praise the Lord for His goodness to you! Now you can hold on to Him with the greatest determination, which becomes stronger with every new release from captivity of sin.

# CHAPTER 4

# GOD'S WAYS VS. HIS ACTS

I am sure you would agree that relationships can be complicated. Just building a friendship with your fellow man can take unusual amounts of energy. How much you are willing to spend building a relationship, shows your attitude toward that person. This is a sorry statement about our society, but is still true. We sometimes pursue those who will bring value into our lives more diligently than those who bring little or no value.

We must examine the term "value" to understand the definition. To some, a neighbor is valued because of the closeness of their location to one's home. Others may devalue a neighbor for the same reason, because they want solitude. As you can see, there are many ingredients involved in human interactions.

## BUILDING A RELATIONSHIP WITH GOD

How do these attitudes affect the relationship that we choose to build with God? Are there selfish motives? If so, do you think our actions fool God? Can you pull the wool over the eyes of Him who can see all? Webster's dictionary describes relationship as "the state of being related by kindred, affinity, or other alliance[9]."

Fortunately, God looks at relationship differently than we do. His desire for us is pure and holy, without impure motives or strings attached. Apart from parenting, there are few examples of a purely love-motivated relationship. That is why I believe God chose to describe Himself as Father.

Our first impressions of someone can influence the relationship we choose to have with that person. If first impressions weigh heavily with you, I would like to encourage you to take a moment to wait for a second impression.

Take, for example, a court judge. Depending on what the case is about, the judge's ruling could include anything from a warning to the death penalty. If we selected only one verdict to consider, and chose to weigh our decision on the judge's character based on that single verdict, we would have a skewed idea of the true character of that judge. If the verdict was for a warning, one interpretation may be the judge was too lenient. If he invoked the death penalty, the interpretation may be that the judge was too severe. Can we, without the proper information covering all the details, come to a correct conclusion about the heart of the judge? I would say, "No!"

When we talk about God with others, have you noticed how many of them have a preconceived idea of who God is? My experience has been that many believe that if God was paying attention at all, He was a vindictive God with a big stick waiting for people to make a mistake, so He could punish them. In this chapter, I will discuss what may skew our relationship with God by using several examples we find in Scripture.

Let me first take you to Exodus 33:

Then the LORD said to Moses, "Depart and go up from here, you and the people whom you have brought out of the land of Egypt, to the land of which I swore to Abraham, Isaac, and Jacob, saying, 'To your descendants I will give it.' And I will send My Angel before you, and I will drive out the Canaanite and the Amorite and the Hittite and the Perizzite and the Hivite and the Jebusite. Go up to a land flowing with milk and honey; for I will not go up in your midst, lest I consume you on the way, for you are a stiff-necked people."

And when the people heard this bad news, they mourned, and no one put on his ornaments. For the LORD had said to Moses, "Say to the children of Israel, 'You are a stiff-necked people. I could come up into your midst in one moment and consume you. Now therefore, take off your ornaments, that I may know what to do to you.'" So the children of Israel stripped themselves of their ornaments by Mount Horeb.

Moses took his tent and pitched it outside the camp, far from the camp, and called it the tabernacle of meeting. And it came to pass that everyone who sought the LORD went out to the tabernacle of meeting which was outside the camp. So it was, whenever Moses went out to the tabernacle, that all the people rose, and each man stood at his tent door and watched Moses until he had gone into the tabernacle. And it came to pass, when Moses entered the tabernacle, that the pillar of cloud descended and stood at the door of the tabernacle, and the Lord talked with Moses. All the people saw the pillar of cloud standing at the tabernacle door, and all the people rose and worshiped, each man in his tent door. So the LORD spoke to Moses face to face, as a man speaks to his friend. And he would return to the camp, but his servant Joshua the son of Nun, a young man, did not depart from the tabernacle.

Then Moses said to the LORD, "See, You say to me, 'Bring up this people.' But You have not let me know whom You will send with me. Yet You have said, 'I know you by name, and you have also found grace in My sight.' Now therefore, I pray, if I have found grace in Your sight, show me now Your way, that I may know You and that I may find grace in Your sight. And consider that this nation is Your people." (vv. 1–13)

God was displeased with Israel because of their sin of disobedience. He told them that He would not go with them to the Promised Land but would send His Angel to accompany them. Israel mourned this news, and as we read, God was to decide what to do with them. This sounds as though God is ferocious, at first glance. Can you see how a reader may interpret God's actions here and choose not to draw near Him?

Moses, at this point, moves and pitches his tent *far* from the camp. If you were an Israelite, how would those actions make you feel? Not only was God saying He did not want to continue going to guide the group, but your leader, Moses, had separated himself from you as well. Imagine the internal stress on the congregation. Besides all these changes, if you desired to seek God, you had to go to the tent of meeting outside camp.

## FACE-TO-FACE OR AT ARM'S LENGTH?

I find it interesting that from this point forward we read that when Moses went into the tent of meeting, all the Israelites would stand at their tent door worshipping God from afar. More important to me is how God talked to Moses face-to-face, "as a man speaks to his friend." We find Israel worshipped from afar and Moses talked with God as a friend. (Take note that Joshua did not leave the tabernacle. This is why I believe God chose him to take Moses' place of leadership as Israel entered the Promised Land.)

God told Moses that he had found grace in God's eyes. Moses pressed this grace as he asked God in verse 13 to, "show me now Your way, that I may know You and that I may find grace in Your sight. And consider that this nation is Your people." Boldness on Moses' part opened the way for him to experience God, as few would ever get the chance. Knowing God's *way* was pivotal to knowing *Him* and reaffirming the grace needed to lead Israel. I believe God fulfilled this request by what Psalms 103 says. "He made known His ways to Moses, His acts to the children of Israel" (v. 7).

The position that the Israelites took, standing at the doors of their tents to worship from afar and not pursuing a closer relationship, limited their interaction and intimacy with God. Joshua was not afraid to go with Moses to the tent of meeting. He did not leave the tent of meeting but remained in God's meeting place, where God talked with Moses.

When Moses entered, the cloud descended and stood at the door. The description of the cloud descending when Moses entered allows us see that there was a time when God lifted from the tent. This may be an insignificant note at this point, but Joshua's example holds a truth for us today. He persisted in getting as close to God as possible, even when God seemed far away.

I believe we have access to God in the same manner. I intently desire to know God and His way. By this type of knowing, I become one in the Spirit with Him. I do not wish to know only His acts, but also His way, or His heart. A pursuit of God with this intent will reward you with a deep intimate knowledge of your heavenly Father.

## God Pursues Us

I was not always so devoted to God. When I was younger in the Lord, I remember the time I felt shortchanged by God and I walked away for several months. I was just starting to know His acts and I was facing some difficulties in my walk. I asked the Lord to stop a particular situation from happening, which did not occur. In my selfish state, I decided to walk away from God. I believed that, "God was not there for me, so why should I be there for Him?" Therefore, off on my merry way I went.

The problem was God would not leave me alone. He dogged me constantly and talked with me, though I did not want to talk to Him. He continued to pour out His mercy and love, despite my rude behavior toward Him. Eventually His love and prodding worked, and I crept into a local church and sat in the second row. Halfway through the sermon, the pastor stopped dead in his tracks and said, "There is someone here this morning who is angry with God and I can't continue until you and God get back together." Naturally, I looked around the room to see whom the pastor was referring to. As God's hand descended upon me, I could feel the fire warming me from head to toe. The call went out again from the pastor and he was determined to wait for the person to step forward.

The presence was so heavy upon me by then, I felt as if I were about to explode! I knew God had been wooing me back to

Himself and this was the moment of restoration of our relationship. I wish I had videotaped what happened next. I burst forward, shoving the chairs out of my way, throwing my hands in the air and shouted, "I give up! It's me!" The flooding of my emotions was beyond anything I had felt until that moment. The bursting of my obstinate heart flung me into His loving arms and I knew I would never walk away again. God's dedication to pursue me at all cost had won me back, bit by bit. God had showed me His way, and I knew His heart and not just His acts.

## HIS ACTS OR HIS WAYS?

Jesus had a similar following that desired only His ability to perform miracles. In John 6, Jesus had fed the 5,000 people, then departed to be alone, sending the disciples before Him. He then walked on the water to catch up to them and together they reached the other side. Let us pick up the story at verse 24:

> When the people therefore saw that Jesus was not there, nor His disciples, they also got into boats and came to Capernaum, seeking Jesus. And when they found Him on the other side of the sea, they said to Him, "Rabbi, when did You come here?" Jesus answered them and said, "Most assuredly, I say to you, you seek Me, not because you saw the signs, but because you ate of the loaves and were filled. Do not labor for the food which perishes, but for the food which endures to everlasting life, which the Son of Man will give you, because God the Father has set His seal on Him."
>
> Then they said to Him, "What shall we do, that we may work the works of God?" Jesus answered and said to them, "This is the work of God, that you believe in Him whom

He sent." Therefore they said to Him, "What sign will You perform then, that we may see it and believe You? What work will You do? Our fathers ate the manna in the desert; as it is written, 'He gave them bread from heaven to eat.'"

Then Jesus said to them, "Most assuredly, I say to you, Moses did not give you the bread from heaven, but My Father gives you the true bread from heaven. For the bread of God is He who comes down from heaven and gives life to the world."

Then they said to Him, "Lord, give us this bread always." And Jesus said to them, "I am the bread of life. He who comes to Me shall never hunger, and he who believes in Me shall never thirst. But I said to you that you have seen Me and yet do not believe. All that the Father gives Me will come to Me, and the one who comes to Me I will by no means cast out. For I have come down from heaven, not to do My own will, but the will of Him who sent Me. This is the will of the Father who sent Me, that of all He has given Me I should lose nothing, but should raise it up at the last day. And this is the will of Him who sent Me, that everyone who sees the Son and believes in Him may have everlasting life; and I will raise him up at the last day."

The Jews then complained about Him, because He said, "I am the bread which came down from heaven." And they said, "Is not this Jesus, the son of Joseph, whose father and mother we know? How is it then that He says, 'I have come down from heaven'?"

Jesus therefore answered and said to them, "Do not murmur among yourselves. No one can come to Me unless the Father who sent Me draws him; and I will raise him up at the last day. It is written in the prophets, 'And they shall

all be taught by God.' Therefore everyone who has heard and learned from the Father comes to Me. Not that anyone has seen the Father, except He who is from God; He has seen the Father. Most assuredly, I say to you, he who believes in Me has everlasting life. I am the bread of life. Your fathers ate the manna in the wilderness, and are dead. This is the bread which comes down from heaven, that one may eat of it and not die. I am the living bread which came down from heaven. If anyone eats of this bread, he will live forever; and the bread that I shall give is My flesh, which I shall give for the life of the world."

The Jews therefore quarreled among themselves, saying, "How can this Man give us His flesh to eat?" Then Jesus said to them, "Most assuredly, I say to you, unless you eat the flesh of the Son of Man and drink His blood, you have no life in you. Whoever eats My flesh and drinks My blood has eternal life, and I will raise him up at the last day. For My flesh is food indeed, and My blood is drink indeed. He who eats My flesh and drinks My blood abides in Me, and I in him. As the living Father sent Me, and I live because of the Father, so he who feeds on Me will live because of Me. This is the bread which came down from heaven—not as your fathers ate the manna, and are dead. He who eats this bread will live forever."

These things He said in the synagogue as He taught in Capernaum. Therefore many of His disciples, when they heard this, said, "This is a hard saying; who can understand it?" When Jesus knew in Himself that His disciples complained about this, He said to them, "Does this offend you? What then if you should see the Son of Man ascend where He was before? It is the Spirit who gives life; the flesh profits nothing. The words that I speak to you are spirit, and they are life. But there are some of you who do not believe." For Jesus knew from the beginning who they were who did not believe, and who would betray Him.

And He said, "Therefore I have said to you that no one can come to Me unless it has been granted to him by My Father." From that time many of His disciples went back and walked with Him no more.

Then Jesus said to the twelve, "Do you also want to go away?" But Simon Peter answered Him, "Lord, to whom shall we go? You have the words of eternal life. Also we have come to believe and know that You are the Christ, the Son of the living God." (vv. 24–69)

We find three distinct types of people in these verses. The first only followed Christ to fill their natural needs or desires, such as food and physical healing. We read of them in verses 22–59. The second, found in verses 60–66, were those disciples who followed and were learning of Jesus' powerful abilities. These disciples knew His acts but not His ways. The final people were the twelve whom had been with Jesus from the beginning. We read of them in verses 67–69.

Peter's response to Christ's question shows how much each of the twelve had invested their time with Jesus. Peter recognized they had been ruined, so to speak, by being with Jesus. I use the word "ruined" because I feel the same as Peter did. In my walk with Jesus, I came to the point of no turning back. I can no longer choose to say, "I'm walking away." I have become so enraptured with Him, I would destroy myself if I attempted to go back to the life I once knew. That life is so foreign to me now, it would be impossible. Going forward with God's guidance is the only choice I have in this life. This choice is the only one I desire, as well.

No greater pleasure can reward me than walking out the plans God has prepared for me. I know without a doubt that all His thoughts are to forge me into the image of His son, Jesus Christ. I believe Peter is speaking similarly when he says, "Also we have come to believe and know that You are the Christ, the Son of the living God" (John 6:69). My heart burns when I read these words, because they resound deeply in my spirit and soul.

To find that you not only believe Jesus, but also know Him, will change everything about who you are! That is what I mean by being "ruined" in Christ. Hallelujah!

## FILTHY RAGS OR RIGHTEOUSNESS?

> Because you say, 'I am rich, have become wealthy, and have need of nothing'—and do not know that you are wretched, miserable, poor, blind, and naked—I counsel you to buy from Me gold refined in the fire, that you may be rich; and white garments, that you may be clothed, that the shame of your nakedness may not be revealed; and anoint your eyes with eye salve, that you may see. (Revelation 3:17–18)

What a tender rebuke from a loving God! It is so much like the little boy who charges into the house, covered from top to bottom with manure, holding up the flowering weeds he picked from the cow pasture triumphantly before his mother. "Look, I picked these for you," he says. He does not realize how dirty he is, all he thinks about is how happy he thinks his mother will be by his gift.

"All my righteousness is as filthy rags," it says in Isaiah 64. "But we are all like an unclean thing, and all our righteousness's are like filthy rags; we all fade as a leaf, and our iniquities, like the wind, have taken us away" (v. 6). The righteousness that comes from Christ makes us "white as snow" (Isaiah 1:18).

My friendship with God (the Father, Son, and Holy Spirit) is above all the stuff that this life may give me. Without Him, I am nothing. Without Him, I am lost. With Him, I can do all things. With Him, I have everything. Pursue Christ! Do whatever you need to find your rest in Him. It is worth it.

## HOLD ON

What does it take to hold on through difficult times?

Now faith is the substance of things hoped for, the evidence of things not seen. For by it the elders obtained a good testimony. By faith we understand that the worlds were framed by the Word of God, so that the things which are seen were not made of things which are visible.

By faith Abel offered to God a more excellent sacrifice than Cain, through which he obtained witness that he was righteous, God testifying of his gifts; and through it he being dead still speaks.

By faith Enoch was taken away so that he did not see death, "and was not found, because God had taken him"; for before he was taken he had this testimony, that he pleased God. But without faith it is impossible to please Him, for he who comes to God must believe that He is, and that He is a rewarder of those who diligently seek Him.

By faith Noah, being divinely warned of things not yet seen, moved with godly fear, prepared an ark for the saving of his household, by which he condemned the world and became heir of the righteousness which is according to faith.

By faith Abraham obeyed when he was called to go out to the place which he would receive as an inheritance. And he went out, not knowing where he was going. By faith he dwelt in the land of promise as in a foreign country, dwelling in tents with Isaac and Jacob, the heirs with him of the same promise; for he waited for the city which has foundations, whose builder and maker is God.

By faith Sarah herself also received strength to conceive seed, and she bore a child when she was past the age, because she judged Him faithful who had promised. Therefore from one man, and him as good as dead, were born as many as the stars of the sky in multitude—innumerable as the sand which is by the seashore. These all died in faith, not having received the promises, but having seen them afar off were assured of them, embraced them and confessed that they were strangers and pilgrims on the earth. For those who say such things declare plainly that they seek a homeland. And truly if they had called to mind that country from which they had come out, they would have had opportunity to return. But now they desire a better, that is, a heavenly country. Therefore God is not ashamed to be called their God, for He has prepared a city for them.

By faith Abraham, when he was tested, offered up Isaac, and he who had received the promises offered up his only begotten son, of whom it was said, "In Isaac your seed shall be called," concluding that God was able to raise him up, even from the dead, from which he also received him in a figurative sense.

By faith Isaac blessed Jacob and Esau concerning things to come.

By faith Jacob, when he was dying, blessed each of the sons of Joseph, and worshiped, leaning on the top of his staff.

By faith Joseph, when he was dying, made mention of the departure of the children of Israel, and gave instructions concerning his bones.

By faith Moses, when he was born, was hidden three months by his parents, because they saw he was a beautiful child; and they were not afraid of the king's command.

By faith Moses, when he became of age, refused to be called the son of Pharaoh's daughter, choosing rather to suffer affliction with the people of God than to enjoy the passing pleasures of sin, esteeming the reproach of Christ greater riches than the treasures in Egypt; for he looked to the reward.

By faith he forsook Egypt, not fearing the wrath of the king; for he endured as seeing Him who is invisible.

By faith he kept the Passover and the sprinkling of blood, lest he who destroyed the firstborn should touch them.

By faith they passed through the Red Sea as by dry land, whereas the Egyptians, attempting to do so, were drowned.

By faith the walls of Jericho fell down after they were encircled for seven days.

By faith the harlot Rahab did not perish with those who did not believe, when she had received the spies with peace.

And what more shall I say? For the time would fail me to tell of Gideon and Barak and Samson and Jephthah, also of David and Samuel and the prophets: who through faith subdued kingdoms, worked righteousness, obtained promises, stopped the mouths of lions, quenched the violence of fire, escaped the edge of the sword, out of weakness were made strong, became valiant in battle, turned to flight the armies of the aliens. Women received their dead raised to life again. And others were tortured, not accepting deliverance, that they might obtain a better resurrection. Still others had trial of mockings and scourgings, yes, and of chains and imprisonment. They were stoned, they were sawn in two, were tempted, were slain with the sword. They wandered about in sheepskins and goatskins, being destitute, afflicted, tormented—of whom the world was not worthy. They wandered in deserts and mountains, in dens and caves of the earth.

And all these, having obtained a good testimony through faith, did not receive the promise, God having provided something better for us, that they should not be made perfect apart from us. (Hebrews 11:1–40)

Faith is what it takes to overcome and please God. Faith is built, like a great city, and has many facets, much like a diamond. Each new challenge has the potential to reflect a different attribute of God's love, abilities, and provision; in other words, all of His benefits.

We, like those in Hebrews, must press on, beyond our understanding to the place of trust, where only God can move. We will get a good testimony by holding on, even if we cannot see the

Lord's answer. Look at verse 39 closely. They "obtained a good testimony through faith, [yet] did not receive the promise."

This is similar to what Christ experienced in Chapter 12 of Hebrews: "Looking unto Jesus, the author and finisher of our faith, who for the joy that was set before Him endured the cross, despising the shame, and has sat down at the right hand of the throne of God" (v. 2). Christ looked at "the joy ... set before Him" just beyond the cross and the shame which He would endure, and pressed on to the joy of the throne where He is now. Christ's faith that the Father would do all He had promised, enabled Him to overcome. We can have that kind of faith.

## THE MIND OF CHRIST

"Jesus, knowing that the Father had given all things into His hands, and that He had come from God and was going to God, rose from supper and laid aside His garments, took a towel and girded Himself" (John 13:3–4). Look at the *"knowing's"* which Jesus had. Jesus *knew* the Father had placed everything into His hands, and He *knew* He had come from God and was going to God. With this knowledge, what did Jesus do? He prepared to finish His ministry to the disciples. He went to work. We can be like Jesus and respond as He did in this life.

This is what the mind of Christ looks like. It says in 1 Corinthians 2:16, "we have the mind of Christ." Do you know that you are walking out God's plan for you? Jesus did. He made it a routine to spend time alone to pray. In those moments, He received the knowing of what was to come.

We need to know what lies ahead. To know this, we must have a routine of making time for prayer or fellowship with God. What a small sacrifice is required, to have such potential for a kingdom-empowered life.

I will close this chapter with this question. What value do you place on God and His presence? Only your life's actions will reveal the truth to you.

# CHAPTER 5

# WHAT DOES A JOURNEY LOOK LIKE?

A journey brings to mind a passage, or traveling from one location to another. I titled this book, *Of Life and Godliness: the Journey,* because of the pilgrimage that is undertaken to get an understanding of both life and godliness. I have been encouraged in my life to enjoy the journey as best as I could, as I learned more about God and myself.

## DO WE KNOW THE PATH?

One of my favorite quotations is, "There is a difference between knowing the path and walking the path[10]." Although most people say that walking the path is better than just knowing the path, I want to put a different twist on it. We find the difference between walking the path and knowing the path in how we interact with our surroundings.

One can meander along completely oblivious to their surroundings (walking the path), plunging headlong into whatever sets itself up to waylay them. What a dangerous prescription for one's life. It is unsettling to me to be blown back and forth by the adverse winds of life like a ship without a rudder. This style of life may be fine for some, but not for many of us travelers.

I wish to be more like those who know the path, knowing where they have been and where it is leading them. I want to be able to share with others the joys and sorrows I have found and savored along the way. To know the path speaks of knowing it so well that you can describe every dip, rise, footfall, or refreshing pool along the way.

## PREPARATION

A journey often takes time to prepare for. We may need to chart the course of the adventure before setting off. We must spend energy to build our endurance for the road that lies ahead. We make plans and spend money on provisions.

In our lives, God is the initiator of our grand pilgrimage, and the guide and financial investor. He Himself sets the times and seasons in our lives. Our lives are not determined by the circumstances we face, but by how we respond to those circumstances. Our attitudes about life most often dictate our response to the conflicts we face. If we are normally a person of faith, then we respond in faith to our challenges.

> And we know that all things work together for good to those who love God, to those who are the called according to His purpose. For whom He foreknew, He also predestined to be conformed to the image of His Son, that He might be the firstborn among many brethren. Moreover

whom He predestined, these He also called; whom He called, these He also justified; and whom He justified, these He also glorified. (Romans 8:28–30)

We must keep the truth of this scripture in mind as we face our challenges. They are what build our character and spiritual stamina. As we stand in faith on God's Word, we prove God is faithful. Here is a terrific scripture to stand on during those times:

Therefore we do not lose heart. Even though our outward man is perishing, yet the inward man is being renewed day by day. For our light affliction, which is but for a moment, is working for us a far more exceeding and eternal weight of glory, while we do not look at the things which are seen, but at the things which are not seen. For the things which are seen are temporary, but the things which are not seen are eternal. (2 Corinthians 4:16–18)

## AS WE TRAVEL

During a journey, we learn something about the destination, and about ourselves. We learn to trust the Lord in new ways as we journey with Him. The challenges we face and the remarkable views we see change us dramatically. The believer's walk is similar, in that there are highs and lows as we go. There are those moments when life comes at us fast and we flinch, awaiting impact. Then there are those special times when we are enraptured in the glory of God, as He reveals His splendor and astounds us.

Journeys through life take on various courses, but there is always the same basic structure. I would like to use Israel's description in Hosea 11 and Ezekiel 16 to describe a journey in life. "When Israel was a child, I loved him, and out of Egypt I called My son" (Hosea 11:1). "I taught Ephraim to walk, taking them by their arms; but they did not know that I healed them" (Hosea 11:3). God chooses us, in our sin, and picks us up and transports us into His kingdom.

## A Lesson From Israel

Now let us study Ezekiel 16. I have inserted my thoughts throughout the passage, found in brackets.

Again the word of the LORD came to me, saying, "Son of man, cause Jerusalem to know her abominations, and say, 'Thus says the Lord GOD to Jerusalem: "Your birth and your nativity are from the land of Canaan; your father was an Amorite and your mother a Hittite. As for your nativity, on the day you were born your navel cord was not cut, nor were you washed in water to cleanse you; you were not rubbed with salt nor wrapped in swaddling cloths." [This describes the complete lack of normal birthing necessities. The umbilical cord was not removed and cleansing of the birthing fluids had not occurred. Neglect is the best description for Israel's state.] No eye pitied you, to do any of these things for you, to have compassion on you; but you were thrown out into the open field, when you yourself were loathed on the day you were born. [This style of abandoning was frequently practiced for reasons of deformity or the inability to care financially for a child.]

"And when I passed by you and saw you struggling in your own blood, I said to you in your blood, 'Live!' Yes, I said to you in your blood, 'Live!' [God saw that death awaited them if He did not intervene.] I made you thrive like a plant in the field; and you grew, matured, and became very beautiful. Your breasts were formed, your hair grew, but you were naked and bare. When I passed by you again and looked upon you, indeed your time was the time of love; so I spread My wing over you and covered your nakedness. [As God nurtured Israel, they flourished under His blessing and He was their covering. The Hebrew word translated "wing" also can be translated "skirt" or "edge," much like what Boaz does to Ruth in Ruth 3:9.] Yes, I swore an oath to you and entered into a covenant with you, and you became Mine," says the Lord GOD. [This is the betrothal of Israel as God's bride. God had reared Israel and had fallen in love with her.]

"Then I washed you in water; yes, I thoroughly washed off your blood, and I anointed you with oil. [This reminds me so much of what Queen Esther experienced before she was presented to the king in Esther 2:12–13.] I clothed you in embroidered cloth and gave you sandals of badger skin; I clothed you with fine linen and covered you with silk. [The clothing speaks of royalty and fineness. The silks and linens are a shadow of priestly garments. The badger skins were the same as the skins that covered the tabernacle of Moses.] I adorned you with ornaments, put bracelets on your wrists, and a chain on your neck. And I put a jewel in your nose, earrings in your ears, and a beautiful crown on your head. [The crown is the final declaration of identity for Israel. She is given the crowning as His queen and all that it entails.] Thus you were adorned with gold and silver, and your clothing was of fine linen, silk, and embroidered cloth. You ate pastry of fine flour, honey, and oil. You were exceedingly beautiful, and succeeded to royalty. Your fame went out among the nations because of your beauty, for it was perfect through My splendor which I had bestowed on you," says the Lord GOD. [Israel, from its' humble beginnings, had now been established and was the jewel of God's eye. He had blessed them with greatness and under Solomon had made them known worldwide. They had become a great nation that was influencing the known world. Something then began to transpire, which God addresses at this point with Israel.]

"But you trusted in your own beauty, played the harlot because of your fame, and poured out your harlotry on everyone passing by who would have it. [Pride had overtaken Israel's heart. Israel believed that she had acquired all the riches by her own abilities. They had forgotten where they had come from.] You took some of your garments and adorned multicolored high places for yourself, and played the harlot on them. Such things should not happen, nor be. You have also taken your beautiful jewelry from My gold and My silver, which I had given you, and made for yourself male images and played the harlot with them. [God was describing the detestable practices that Israel had begun.] You took your embroidered garments and covered them, and you set My oil and My incense before them. Also My food which I gave you—the pastry of fine flour, oil, and honey which I fed you—you set it before them as sweet incense; and so it was," says the Lord GOD. [To add insult to injury, they were taking the incense and oil for the Temple and using it in idol worship.] "Moreover you took your sons and your daughters, whom you bore to Me, and these you sacrificed to them to be devoured. Were your acts of harlotry a small matter, that you have slain My children and offered them up to them by causing them to pass through the fire? [Israel had fallen so deep into idolatry that they were sacrificing their children to inanimate idols.] And in all your abominations and acts of harlotry you did not remember the days of your youth, when you were naked and bare, struggling in your blood.

"Then it was so, after all your wickedness—'Woe, woe to you!' says the Lord GOD—that you also built for yourself a shrine, and made a high place for yourself in every street. You built your high places at the head of every road, and made your beauty to be abhorred. You offered yourself to everyone who passed by, and multiplied your acts of harlotry. You also committed harlotry with the Egyptians, your very fleshly neighbors, and increased your acts of harlotry to provoke Me to anger. Behold, therefore, I stretched out My hand against you, diminished your allotment, and gave you up to the will of those who hate you, the daughters of the Philistines, who were ashamed of your lewd behavior. You also played the harlot with the Assyrians, because you were insatiable; indeed you played the harlot with them and still were not satisfied. Moreover you multiplied your acts of harlotry as far as the land of the trader, Chaldea; and even then you were not satisfied. How degenerate is your heart!" says the Lord GOD, "seeing you do all these things, the deeds of a brazen harlot.

"You erected your shrine at the head of every road, and built your high place in every street. Yet you were not like a harlot, because you scorned payment. You are an adulterous wife, who takes strangers instead of her husband. Men make payment to all harlots, but you made your payments to all your lovers, and hired them to come to you from all around for your harlotry. You are the opposite of other women in your harlotry, because no one solicited you to be a harlot. In that you gave payment but no payment was given you, therefore you are the opposite."

'Now then, O harlot, hear the word of the LORD! [God is about to get Israel's attention.] Thus says the Lord GOD: "Because your filthiness was poured out and your nakedness uncovered in your harlotry with your lovers, and with all your abominable idols, and because of the blood of your children which you gave to them, surely, therefore, I will gather all your lovers with whom you took pleasure, all those you loved, and all those you hated; I will gather them from all around against you and will uncover your nakedness to them, that they may see all your nakedness. And I will judge you as women who break wedlock or shed blood are judged; I will bring blood upon you in fury and jealousy. I will also give you into their hand, and they shall throw down your shrines and break down your high places. They shall also strip you of your clothes, take your beautiful jewelry, and leave you naked and bare. The countries that Israel hated as well as those whom Israel trusted will turn on them and take away their riches. They shall also bring up an assembly against you, and they shall stone you with stones and thrust you through with their swords. They shall burn your houses with fire, and execute judgments on you in the sight of many women; and I will make you cease playing the harlot, and you shall no longer hire lovers. So I will lay to rest My fury toward you, and My jealousy shall depart from you. I will be quiet, and be angry no more. [This is not forgiveness but a turning over of Israel for destruction, very similar to turning a sinful brother over to Satan. "of whom are Hymenaeus and Alexander, whom I delivered to Satan that they may learn not to blaspheme" (1 Timothy 1:20).] Because you did not remember the days of your youth, but agitated Me with all these things, surely I will also recompense your deeds on your own head," says the Lord GOD. "And you shall not commit lewdness in addition to all your abominations.

"Indeed everyone who quotes proverbs will use this proverb against you: 'Like mother, like daughter!' You are your mother's daughter, loathing husband and children; and you are the sister of your sisters, who loathed their husbands and children; your mother was a Hittite and your father an Amorite. Your elder sister is Samaria, who dwells with her daughters to the north of you; and your younger sister, who dwells to the south of you, is Sodom and her daughters. You did not walk in their ways nor act according to their abominations; but, as if that were too little, you became more corrupt than they in all your ways. As I live," says the Lord GOD, "neither your sister Sodom nor her daughters have done as you and your daughters have done. [God is about to go into detail in comparing Israel with those around her.] Look, this was the iniquity of your sister Sodom: She and her daughter had pride, fullness of food, and abundance of idleness; neither did she strengthen the hand of the poor and needy. And they were haughty and committed abomination before Me; therefore I took them away as I saw fit. Samaria did not commit half of your sins; but you have multiplied your abominations more than they, and have justified your sisters by all the abominations which you have done. You who judged your sisters, bear your own shame also, because the sins which you committed were more abominable than theirs; they are more righteous than you. Yes, be disgraced also, and bear your own shame, because you justified your sisters.

"When I bring back their captives, the captives of Sodom and her daughters, and the captives of Samaria and her daughters, then I will also bring back the captives of your captivity among them, that you may bear your own shame and be disgraced by all that you did when you comforted them. When your sisters, Sodom and her daughters, return to their former state, and Samaria and her daughters return to their former state, then you and your daughters will return to your former state. For your sister Sodom was not a byword in your mouth in the days of your pride, before your wickedness was uncovered. It was like the time of the reproach of the daughters of Syria and all those around her, and of the daughters of the Philistines, who despise you everywhere. You have paid for your lewdness and your abominations," says the LORD. For thus says the Lord GOD: "I will deal with you as you have done, who despised the oath by breaking the covenant.

"Nevertheless I will remember My covenant with you in the days of your youth, and I will establish an everlasting covenant with you. [God is saying, "Even though you forgot your covenant with Me, I will remember and I will establish an everlasting covenant with you." What a powerful statement toward Israel.] Then you will remember your ways and be ashamed, when you receive your older and your younger sisters; for I will give them to you for daughters, but not because of My covenant with you. And I will establish My covenant with you. Then you shall know that

I am the LORD, that you may remember and be ashamed, and never open your mouth anymore because of your shame, when I provide you an atonement for all you have done," says the Lord GOD.' (vv. 1–63)

I included this entire passage to show you that God, standing outside time, treats people as one entity. You, as an individual, are important, but you are part of a body, and your individual significance adds to the importance of the whole. Just as God Himself had nurtured and established Israel as a nation of individuals, God is now nurturing us, the Body of Christ.

God had given Israel lesson after lesson, only to have future generations forget what He had taught them. If you study the Old Testament, you find how one generation may have followed God zealously, and the next generation would turn the opposite direction toward paganism and idolatry. Each generation stands on the spiritual shoulders of the previous generations.

I believe that just as God nurtured Israel, He also takes each of us and trains us up for greatness in His kingdom. We cannot afford as a generation to forget what God has taught us. Future generations depend on our obedience.

Israel went so far as to cause God to present her with a certificate of divorce.

The LORD said also to me in the days of Josiah the king: "Have you seen what backsliding Israel has done? She has gone up on every high mountain and under every green tree, and there played the harlot. And I said, after she had done all these things, 'Return to Me.' But she did not return. And her treacherous sister Judah saw it. Then I saw that for all the causes for which backsliding Israel had committed adultery, I had put her away and given her a certificate of divorce; yet her treacherous sister Judah did not fear, but went and played the harlot also. So it came to pass, through her casual harlotry, that she defiled the land and committed adultery with stones and trees. And yet for all this her treacherous sister Judah has not turned to Me with her whole heart, but in pretense," says the LORD. Then the LORD said to me, "Backsliding Israel has shown herself more righteous than treacherous Judah." (Jeremiah 3:6–11)

Even though Israel fell into adultery, God never fully rejected them as a people. I want to make clear that the church of today has not replaced them—Israel is still God's chosen people.

## The Birth of the Church

Here is another example of how God is nurturing a people. This story begins in Acts 2:

When the Day of Pentecost had fully come, they were all with one accord in one place. And suddenly there came a sound from heaven, as of a rushing mighty wind, and it filled the whole house where they were sitting. Then there appeared to them divided tongues, as of fire, and one sat upon each of them. And they were all filled with the Holy Spirit and began to speak with other tongues, as the Spirit gave them utterance. (vv. 1–4)

The birthing of the church occurred that day. God founded the church similarly to the way He founded Israel. Peter stood and addressed this event with a powerfully anointed declaration, under the anointing of the Spirit. The outcome was the salvation of some three-thousand people on the day of Pentecost.

Before that time, the Jews historically celebrated this day of Pentecost as a commemoration of the delivery of the Law at Sinai to Moses, and as the Day of First Fruits (or the Feast of Harvest.) I believe there is a correlation here to the three thousand lost in death by the sons of Levi in Exodus 32:26–28, at the time of the giving of the Law. There is also a correlation to the Day of First Fruits, because this represents the first fruits (the beginning) of the birth of the church.

"Not that we are sufficient of ourselves to think of anything as being from ourselves, but our sufficiency is from God, who also made us sufficient as ministers of the new covenant, not of the letter but of the Spirit; for the letter kills, but the Spirit gives life" (2 Corinthians 3:5–6). Just as the three-thousand perished at the delivery of the Law, here the Holy Spirit delivered three thousand from death to life.

## THE MODERN CHURCH

Without going into depth about church history, I would like to give a brief overview of how the church matured through the ages. From the church's birth at Pentecost, she continued to grow as Christ added to His church. The conversion of many Gentiles (non-Jews) swelled the number of this new group daily. The references found in the book of Acts tell of a Spirit-led explosion of converts.

From this small group of prayerful, upper-room faithful, came a world-sweeping move of God. As the centuries passed, many came to feel the call of God. I could talk of Constantine or Gregory the Great. I could discuss the Medieval times or the separation of the Eastern and Western churches. We could go on to speak of

The Reformation, Martin Luther, and John Wycliffe, John Calvin or John Wesley and their movements. If you have ever studied their teachings, you can see how God moved on humanity to reveal distinct attributes of Himself. I would encourage you to study these events and people for yourself, and to become educated about how the church survived through the ages of time.

There have been many waves of awakening which have visited our country in the last couple of centuries. People like Jonathan Edwards and George Whitefield appeared in the 1700s. The Cane Ridge revival and the upstate New York revivals influenced much of the northeastern part of the United States during the early 1800s. In the 1900s, the ground began to shake in a small building at 312 Azusa Street, Los Angeles, California. I encourage you to do some of your own research about these great outpourings. The Lord was not only working on this continent, but also on the rest of the world. Evan Roberts was a humble man used by God to touch a nation in the Welsh Revival.

Here in the United States during the twentieth century, both men and women were receiving powerful anointings from God. These great mothers and fathers of the faith set a foundation for the Jesus movement of the 1970s. People like Maria Woodworth-Etter, A. A. Allen, Charles F. Parham, Jack Coe, William Branham, Kathryn Kuhlman, Aimee Semple McPherson, John G. Lake and Smith Wigglesworth, affected regions of not only America but the world. From the Pentecostal movement to the Charismatic movement in our recent years, I believe God is showing forth who He is and training His Bride.

## MATURING THE CHURCH

God is training the Church today, just as He did with Israel in years past. He has been revealing truth, "precept on precept, line upon line" (Isaiah 28:10), and the church has been listening. Just as God provided a washing of Israel from its blood in Ezekiel 16:9, I believe Jesus washes the church with His Word. "That He might sanctify and cleanse her with the washing of water by the word, that He might present her to Himself a glorious church, not having spot or wrinkle or any such thing, but that she should be holy and without blemish" (Ephesians 5:26–27).

As God revealed truth to His men and women across the ages, many believed they had received the final truth and built a denomination around that truth. I believe that God continues to reveal truth, to bring the church to maturity.

God often brings revelation to change the direction of His people. God brought revelation to Peter in Acts 11:

Now the apostles and brethren who were in Judea heard that the Gentiles had also received the word of God. And when Peter came up to Jerusalem, those of the circumcision contended with him, saying, "You went in to uncircumcised men and ate with them!" But Peter explained it to them in order from the beginning, saying: "I was in the city of Joppa praying; and in a trance I saw a vision, an object descending like a great sheet, let down from heaven by four corners; and it came to me. When I observed it intently and considered, I saw four-footed animals of the earth, wild beasts, creeping things, and birds of the air. And I heard a voice saying to me, 'Rise, Peter; kill and eat.' But I said, 'Not so, Lord! For nothing common or unclean has at any time entered my mouth.' But the voice answered me again from heaven, 'What God has cleansed you must not call common.' Now this was done three times, and all were drawn up again into heaven. At that very moment, three men stood before the house where I was, having been sent to me from Caesarea. Then the Spirit told me to go with them, doubting nothing. Moreover these six brethren accompanied me, and we entered the man's house. And he told us how he had seen an angel standing in his house, who said to him, 'Send men to Joppa, and call for Simon whose surname is Peter, who will tell you words by which you and all your household will be saved.' And as I began to speak, the Holy Spirit fell upon them, as upon us at the beginning. Then I remembered the word of the Lord, how He said, 'John indeed baptized with water, but you shall be baptized with the Holy Spirit.' If therefore God gave them the same gift as He gave us when we believed on the Lord Jesus Christ, who was I that I could withstand God?" When they heard these things they became silent; and they glorified God, saying, "Then God has also granted to the Gentiles repentance to life." (vv. 1–18)

This vision was not about what was to be eaten, but about including Gentile believers into the church. Until that time, the disciples, and even Jesus (with one exception in Matthew 15:21–28), had only preached salvation to and ministered to the Jews. They held the traditional, Old Testament understanding that the Jews were God's only chosen people, and the only people offered the chance to eternal salvation. In this scripture, God is giving them a new revelation that now (since the death and resurrection of Jesus), they were to share the salvation message with the Gentiles, as well. This was such a significant change from their belief system, that God had to tell Peter three times before he would believe it.

This revelation changed what Peter had believed about God's attitude toward the Gentiles and opened the door, which eventually allowed our invitation as non-Jewish Gentiles into "repentance to life."

"And as I began to speak, the Holy Spirit fell upon them, as upon us at the beginning. Then I remembered the word of the Lord, how He said, 'John indeed baptized with water, but you shall be baptized with the Holy Spirit.' If therefore God gave them the same gift as He gave us when we believed on the Lord Jesus Christ, who was I that I could withstand God?" When they heard these things they became silent; and they glorified God, saying, "Then God has also granted to the Gentiles repentance to life." (Acts 11:15–18)

As previously stated, denominations often set up their doctrines around the revelations that they have received, and resist accepting new beliefs. I believe God is constantly adding new blessings of understanding to His Body, the maturing young woman He calls His church. Just as God described Israel as thriving like a plant in the field, and that she grew, matured, and became beautiful, I see Him saying the same about the church.

Looking back at Ezekiel 16, what if, as I believe, the embroidered cloth and badger skin sandals were not tangible items, but symbolic of God's gifts to His people? What if the silver, gold, fine linen and silks, ornaments, bracelets, and jewels that God gave Israel, also represent the great men and women who have heralded His Word to the world over the years? What would happen if we placed each truth that God has revealed into today's church and layered them as embellishments on a beautiful bride? I believe we would see the establishment and maturing of a lovely, living, breathing Bride of Christ. God does not describe His Body as divided, but united! "Till we all come to the unity of the faith and of the knowledge of the Son of God, to a perfect man, to the measure of the stature of the fullness of Christ" (Ephesians 4:13). This may not sound like the church that you know, but this is how God's Word describes it.

What if the "fine pastry of honey and oil" given to us, as described in Ezekiel 16:13, represented God's Word or revelations through the great men and women of the church? Have we created a type of idol with our divisive stance of being correct above all others with our doctrines, which divide the Body of Christ? Have we set God's food, His Word, before those *idols of doctrines* as a sweet offering, like Ezekiel 16:19? Are we sacrificing the church, Christ's body, as in Ezekiel 16:20, to hold on to a doctrine meant to bring wisdom, not division? This is a hard word, and may challenge your belief system, but if your belief system were contrary to God's plans, wouldn't you want to know?

I believe the church was birthed in unity and was meant to continue in unity, as we become "a perfect man," in "the full stature of Christ" (Ephesians 4:13). What would the Body of Christ look like if it embraced this idea? Would today's leaders send new letters that sound like the Books that the Apostle Paul wrote to the Church of Rome, Corinth, or even Ephesus? Would we be talking about the church of Beijing, London, Sydney, or New York? What an exciting prospect! Just as God the Father made Israel His queen and wife, Christ will have a Bride, the church.

Husbands, love your wives, just as Christ also loved the church and gave Himself for her, that He might sanctify and cleanse her with the washing of water by the word, that He might present her to Himself a glorious church, not having spot or wrinkle or any such thing, but that she should be holy and without blemish. (Ephesians 5:25–27)

## CHURCH OF THE LAST HOUR

I would like to close this chapter with this analogy from Matthew 20:

For the kingdom of heaven is like a landowner who went out early in the morning to hire laborers for his vineyard. Now when he had agreed with the laborers for a denarius a day, he sent them into his vineyard. And he went out about the third hour and saw others standing idle in the marketplace, and said to them, "You also go into the vineyard, and whatever is right I will give you." So they went.

Again he went out about the sixth and the ninth hour, and did likewise. And about the eleventh hour he went out and found others standing idle, and said to them, "Why have you been standing here idle all day?" They said to him, "Because no one hired us." He said to them, "You also go into the vineyard, and whatever is right you will receive."

So when evening had come, the owner of the vineyard said to his steward, "Call the laborers and give them their wages, beginning with the last to the first." And when those came who were hired about the eleventh hour, they each received a denarius. But when the first came, they supposed that they would receive more; and they likewise received each a denarius. And when they had received it, they complained against the landowner, saying, "These last men have worked only one hour, and you made them equal to us who have borne the burden and the heat of the day."

But he answered one of them and said, "Friend, I am doing you no wrong. Did you not agree with me for a denarius? Take what is yours and go your way. I wish to give to this last man the same as to you. Is it not lawful for me to do what I wish with my own things? Or is your eye evil because I am good?" So the last will be first, and the first last. For many are called, but few chosen. (vv. 1–16)

I believe this is a perfect picture of the church. Across the ages, many have answered the call to work in God's vineyard and have given their lives. Well-known men and women, and many more whose names are unknown, have influenced the world for our King. Today we benefit from the revelations and progressive anointings of those men and women, who have "borne the burden and the heat of the day" for the Kingdom.

I believe the *"last man"* of this scripture represents the church of the last hour. I also believe that we are in that last hour, and even the last moments, before the return of our glorious King Jesus! If I am correct, we will receive the full blessing of seeing the coming of Christ in our lifetime.

The plowing and planting of our spiritual fathers and mothers have given us the potential of unprecedented harvest for the kingdom. Just as the vineyard owner said, "I wish to give to this last man *the same* as to you," I believe Jesus is saying this to us today. "And he who reaps receives wages, and gathers fruit for eternal life, that both he who sows and he who reaps may rejoice together. For in this the saying is true: 'One sows and another reaps.' I sent you to reap that for which you have not labored;

others have labored, and you have entered into their labors" (John 4:36–38). God will pour out on us as we labor under His direction.

We are flourishing, not because of what we have done, but because of what God has prepared for us to do. Those raised in the church may well be surprised when the newly saved surpass them with their zeal for God's Kingdom. The hearts of some in the church may reflect the envy found in the first hired, at the time of payment in Matthew 20:11–12, as these new Christians' anointings shine forth. We need to rejoice that God's grace has been extended to all new believers. God sees us as equal in His Kingdom, so we have no legitimate reason to question His blessings upon others.

We must embrace the gift of salvation and press on toward our individual rewards for our service to the kingdom. Our salvation and rewards are two separate things. Our salvation provides entry *into* the Kingdom but our crowns are the rewards for service *to* the Kingdom. Ultimately, we will cast our crowns at the foot of the throne, according to Revelation 4:10.

Because we are the *Church of the last hour,* let us go forward and be diligent in the task of advancing God's Kingdom. May the laborers described in Luke 10:2 aid us in our quest. "The harvest ... is great," and "the laborers are few," and time is short. I pray God's blessing on the work of our hands as we advance His Kingdom.

As I conclude this chapter, consider the attributes of the church of the last hour and the workings of the Holy Spirit. The scriptures say that Jesus will find faith and a powerful Spirit-led church when He returns. My challenge to you is, "Let's get to the harvest." Let the church rise and move as Christ's body on the earth, preparing for our King's return!

"For I consider that the sufferings of this present time are not worthy to be compared with the glory which shall be revealed in us. For the earnest expectation of the creation eagerly waits for the revealing of the sons of God" (Romans 8:18–19). Let the "revealing of the Sons of God" begin.

The journey of which God has been leading His church has brought us to the place of being revealed in power and authority. As the sons of God break forth from the training and preparation to reign with Christ, we will be able to say, "But for the glory that is to be revealed within us, we endured the shame and suffering in life." May you find the joys of the journey, and new levels of trust with God at your side!

# CHAPTER 6

# OF LIFE . . .

Our lives are established by God. ". . . Unless the LORD builds the house, They labor in vain who build it; Unless the LORD guards the city, The watchman stays awake in vain" (Psalm 127:1).

## BUILDING OUR HOUSES

We can compare the building of our lives to the building of a house. Great preparation and planning go into each of them, and they both require a strong foundation as well. Building your life on Jesus will guarantee a successful life.

We do not want our labors to be useless, so we must trust God to build us as He sees fit. "Through wisdom a house is built, and by understanding it is established; by knowledge the rooms are filled with all precious and pleasant riches" (Proverbs 24:3–4). The house in this scripture represents one's life. "The fear of the Lord is the beginning of Wisdom: A good understanding have those who do His commandments" (Psalms 111:10). The fear of the Lord, which is wisdom, builds our life (our house) upon a firm foundation.

"By understanding [our lives are] established." In other words, God provides us with all the necessities of life and godliness. By our knowledge of God, our "rooms," or daily life, are filled with "precious and pleasant riches." Those many blessings occur as we walk in the blessings of the Lord.

## BLESSINGS OVERTAKE US

This scripture best represents what I mean by being "blessed." "And all these blessings shall come upon you and overtake you, because you obey the voice of the LORD your God" (Deuteronomy 28:2). Blessings work like this. As we obey the voice of the Lord and walk out His calling upon our lives, blessings fall upon us. In addition to these blessings, there are those that will overtake us.

Now picture this in your mind. You are walking the path of the Lord, stepping into the steps directed by Him. There are divine blessings raining down upon you from heaven as Jesus Himself is interceding for your life and destiny. At the same time a tidal wave of blessings are building and overtaking you from behind. They burst over you and add to the blessings already upon you. There is no way you can out-run the purposes and blessings of God for your life. You can only stop them dead in their tracks by disobeying the Lord.

## LIFE

With this awareness of understanding and knowledge, let us proceed to discuss life. Webster's New World Dictionary defines "life" this way: "the time a person or thing is alive or exists, or a specific portion of such time", "an individual's animate existence," and "the existence of the soul[11]." In other words, life is simply being alive or existing, both in our body and in our soul or spirit.

Peter Mark Roget shows a high regard for life by listing "life" in his International Thesaurus under the heading of "existence," and placing it in the very first entry of the entire thesaurus[12]. God Himself breathed life into Adam, the very first human, in Genesis 2:7.

Life incorporates so much more than can be mentioned in a few sentences or in the number of days that one exists upon the earth. I have heard it said that the dates chiseled into a headstone are the bookends of a life lived between them. The value of life also holds much more than what our society dictates to us.

Just imagine what life would be like without one particular person, any one person. The influence of one person, whether for good or bad, can affect the world in some way or other. Look at the genealogy of Jesus, which is found in both Matthew and Luke:

The book of the genealogy of Jesus Christ, the Son of David, the Son of Abraham: Abraham begot Isaac, Isaac begot Jacob, and Jacob begot Judah and his brothers. Judah begot Perez and Zerah by Tamar, Perez begot Hezron, and Hezron begot Ram. Ram begot Amminadab, Amminadab begot Nahshon, and Nahshon begot Salmon. Salmon begot Boaz by Rahab, Boaz begot Obed by Ruth, Obed begot Jesse, and Jesse begot David the king. David the king begot Solomon by her who had been the wife of Uriah.

Solomon begot Rehoboam, Rehoboam begot Abijah, and Abijah begot Asa. Asa begot Jehoshaphat, Jehoshaphat begot Joram, and Joram begot Uzziah. Uzziah begot

Jotham, Jotham begot Ahaz, and Ahaz begot Hezekiah. Hezekiah begot Manasseh, Manasseh begot Amon, and Amon begot Josiah. Josiah begot Jeconiah and his brothers about the time they were carried away to Babylon.

And after they were brought to Babylon, Jeconiah begot Shealtiel, and Shealtiel begot Zerubbabel. Zerubbabel begot Abiud, Abiud begot Eliakim, and Eliakim begot Azor. Azor begot Zadok, Zadok begot Achim, and Achim begot Eliud. Eliud begot Eleazar, Eleazar begot Matthan, and Matthan begot Jacob.

And Jacob begot Joseph the husband of Mary, of whom was born Jesus who is called Christ. So all the generations from Abraham to David are fourteen generations, from David until the captivity in Babylon are fourteen generations, and from the captivity in Babylon until the Christ are fourteen generations. (Matthew 1:1–17)

Now Jesus Himself began His ministry at about thirty years of age, being (as was supposed) the son of Joseph, the son of Heli, the son of Matthat, the son of Levi, the son of Melchi, the son of Janna, the son of Joseph, the son of Mattathiah, the son of Amos, the son of Nahum, the son of Esli, the son of Naggai, the son of Maath, the son of Mattathiah, the son of Semei, the son of Joseph, the son of Judah, the son of Joannas, the son of Rhesa, the son of Zerubbabel, the son of Shealtiel, the son of Neri, the son of Melchi, the son of Addi, the son of Cosam, the son of Elmodam, the son of Er, the son of Jose, the son of Eliezer, the son of Jorim, the son of Matthat, the son of Levi, the son of Simeon, the son of Judah, the son of Joseph, the son of Jonan, the son of Eliakim, the son of Melea, the son of

Menan, the son of Mattathah, the son of Nathan, the son of David, the son of Jesse, the son of Obed, the son of Boaz, the son of Salmon, the son of Nahshon, the son of Amminadab, the son of Ram, the son of Hezron, the son of Perez, the son of Judah, the son of Jacob, the son of Isaac, the son of Abraham, the son of Terah, the son of Nahor, the son of Serug, the son of Reu, the son of Peleg, the son of Eber, the son of Shelah, the son of Cainan, the son of Arphaxad, the son of Shem, the son of Noah, the son of Lamech, the son of Methuselah, the son of Enoch, the son of Jared, the son of Mahalalel, the son of Cainan, the son of Enos, the son of Seth, the son of Adam, the son of God. (Luke 3:23–38)

These names were not just faceless people from ages ago, but a lineage of the King of Kings and Lord of Lords. Just the loss of one person in this lineage would be significant.

The names of the women listed in Matthew, for example, are Tamar, Rahab, Ruth, and "Her who had been the wife of Uriah" (Bathsheba). These women were meaningful because of their diverse background. The extreme differences between a young widow impregnated by her father-in-law, a prostitute, an adulteress, and a king's wife are found within Jesus' bloodline and demonstrate that all have an important part to play in His arrival upon the earth.

## WE ARE IMPORTANT

As children of God, our lives hold a significance we may never realize. Many remember the famous men and women of this world, but few know who Henry and Hannah Roberts were. These two were the parents of the Welsh Revivalist, Evan John Roberts.[13]

Simon and Phyllis Seymour were former slaves, but they were the parents of William J Seymour of Azusa Street Mission.[14]

Another example is John and Martha Wigglesworth. These two people, though not believers, were the parents of the great man of God, Smith Wigglesworth.[15]

The seeds sown by the witness of our lives, just like Roberts, Seymour, and Wigglesworth, have the potential of changing nations as well as families. Never dismiss the importance of your life or those you may touch. Jesus gave His life for you, so live up to the potential He sees in you! All these men and women lived a life fired with revelation from God—so must we!

## THE SECRETS OF GOD

One of the most powerful life-changing revelations I have received from the Spirit is in Deuteronomy 29. "The secret things belong to the LORD our God, but those things which are revealed belong to us and to our children forever, that we may do all the words of this law" (v. 29).

God's love for me has inspired me to pursue the Lord continually. I do not pursue Him for sake of revelation alone, but revelation is a by-product of our relationship. I learn God's ways, not just His actions, as I spend time in prayer, meditation on His Word, and in times of praise and worship. He captures my attitudes and heart, and in exchange I receive His heart and what moves Him.

"That their hearts may be encouraged, being knit together in love, and attaining to all riches of the full assurance of understanding, to the knowledge of the mystery of God, both of the Father and of Christ, in whom are hidden all the treasures of wisdom and knowledge" (Colossians 2:2–3). God has many secrets and mysteries that are available for discovery by those who seek Him.

Let a man so consider us, as servants of Christ and stewards of the mysteries of God. Moreover, it is required in stewards that one be found faithful. But with me it is a very small thing that I should be judged by you or by a human court. In fact, I do not even judge myself. For I know nothing against myself, yet I am not justified by this; but He who judges me is the Lord. Therefore judge nothing before the time, until the Lord comes, who will both bring to light the hidden things of darkness and reveal the counsels of the hearts. Then each one's praise will come from God. (1 Corinthians 4:1–5)

The mysteries of God are for those who desire wisdom and understanding. "Whatever I tell you in the dark, speak in the light; and what you hear in the ear, preach on the housetops" (Matthew 10:27). When we receive revelations from God, we are not to keep them to ourselves, but to share them with those around us.

I seek God within my intimate times of prayer, praise, and worship and the reading of His Word. The apostle John puts it like this:

That which was from the beginning, which we have heard, which we have seen with our eyes, which we have looked upon, and our hands have handled, concerning the Word of life—the life was manifested, and we have seen, and bear witness, and declare to you that eternal life which was with the Father and was manifested to us—that which we have seen and heard we declare to you, that you also may have fellowship with us; and truly our fellowship is with the Father and with His Son Jesus Christ. And these things we write to you that your joy may be full. (1 John 1:1–4)

We must handle God's Word in the same way, in order to know Him. Notice how many times the words "heard," "seen," "looked upon," "handled," and "manifested" are used in this scripture. These are action words and show that they intimately knew who Jesus was. First-hand knowledge gave the apostles boldness because they knew beyond a shadow of doubt Jesus was the true savior. We must also base our faith on first-hand knowledge of Christ. We do not get to heaven on someone else's faith or salvation. God desires for us to know Him personally.

## REVELATIONS FROM GOD

This style of pursuit of God creates fellowship, as well as spiritual endurance. As God reveals truth to us, it takes root in our hearts and becomes a part of our belief system. This normally occurs either in prayer time or through daily Bible reading. The truth that He reveals to us mixes with faith and we take ownership of the revelation.

Let me share a simple example of what I am describing. "And the LORD, He is the one who goes before you. He will be with you, He will not leave you nor forsake you; do not fear nor be dismayed" (Deuteronomy 31:8). I know that this scripture speaks directly to me, and I base my spiritual life upon it. I have added another scripture as well, to give me a strong base for facing all the challenges in life. "For I know the thoughts that I think toward you, says the LORD, thoughts of peace and not of evil, to give you a future and a hope" (Jeremiah 29:11). These two scriptures have worked hand-in-hand to help me "set my face like flint" (Isaiah 50:7) in the direction of God's call upon my life.

We live out our lives with the revelations God has blessed us with. Those around us witness the impact those truths have on our daily lives, and are touched. As we live the overcoming life, many will desire to learn more about those secrets that influence our lives. The draw of the Spirit upon those who observe our lives gives opportunity to fulfill the great commission Christ Jesus has given us by sharing Him with them. We advance the kingdom each time we share what God has done in our lives.

The best part of Deuteronomy 29:29 is the last line, "That we may do all the words of this law." God's desire for us to succeed is so profound that He reveals truth to us, the secrets of success of the Kingdom. His Holy Spirit then establishes these revelations within our lives, as we surrender to His will.

## THE KINGDOM WITHIN US

Because of the establishment of the Kingdom within us, we begin to experience the overcoming life. As we are transformed into the likeness of God's Son, as stated in 2 Corinthians 3:18, we lose the drive to fulfill the desires of the flesh. The transformation to Christ-likeness empowers us to live a sinless life. "Whoever has been born of God does not sin, for His seed remains in him; and he cannot sin, because he has been born of God" (1 John 3:9).

The understanding of the Kingdom of God is one of God's secrets and mysteries. "And He said to them, 'To you it has been given to know the mystery of the kingdom of God; but to those who are outside, all things come in parables'" (Mark 4:11). Studying Scripture is the best place to see the work of the Kingdom in a person's life.

## BE FRUITFUL

Then He taught them many things by parables, and said to them in His teaching: "Listen! Behold, a sower went out to sow. And it happened, as he sowed, that some seed fell by the wayside; and the birds of the air came and devoured it.

Some fell on stony ground, where it did not have much earth; and immediately it sprang up because it had no depth of earth. But when the sun was up it was scorched, and because it had no root it withered away. And some seed fell among thorns; and the thorns grew up and choked it, and it yielded no crop. But other seed fell on good ground and yielded a crop that sprang up, increased and produced: some thirtyfold, some sixty, and some a hundred." And He said to them, "He who has ears to hear, let him hear!"

But when He was alone, those around Him with the twelve asked Him about the parable. And He said to them, "To you it has been given to know the mystery of the kingdom of God; but to those who are outside, all things come in parables, so that 'Seeing they may see and not perceive, And hearing they may hear and not understand; Lest they should turn, And their sins be forgiven them.'"

And He said to them, "Do you not understand this parable? How then will you understand all the parables? The sower sows the word. And these are the ones by the wayside where the word is sown. When they hear, Satan comes immediately and takes away the word that was sown in their hearts.

"These likewise are the ones sown on stony ground who, when they hear the word, immediately receive it with gladness; and they have no root in themselves, and so endure only for a time. Afterward, when tribulation or persecution arises for the word's sake, immediately they stumble.

"Now these are the ones sown among thorns; they are the ones who hear the word, and the cares of this world, the deceitfulness of riches, and the desires for other things entering in choke the word, and it becomes unfruitful. But these are the ones sown on good ground, those who hear the word, accept it, and bear fruit: some thirtyfold, some sixty, and some a hundred." (Mark 4:2–20)

The factors that determine fruitfulness are the revelations we have from God and their influence in our daily walk. As we hear the Word, or those things revealed of God, and accept it as truth, we bear fruit in our lives. God has destined you to be fruitful.

"By this My Father is glorified, that you bear much fruit; so you will be My disciples" (John 15:8). This scripture is saying that when we bear much fruit, we bring glory to the Father. I read it like this, "Because you bear tons of fruit for the glory of my Father, I have chosen you to be my disciples." His choice comes from His desire to see glory lavished upon the Father through our fruitfulness.

## KNOWLEDGE FROM RELATIONSHIP

"As His divine power has given to us all things that pertain to life and godliness, through the knowledge of Him who called us by glory and virtue" (2 Peter 1:3). God's divine power is awesome! Nothing can resist His power—it is unstoppable! That power pours forth to provide us with all the necessities for life and godliness, but it comes through knowledge of Him.

Several scriptures show what knowledge of Him looks like. These scriptures are all based on a face-to-face relationship with God. There is no other way to know Him and all that He is, apart from this style of relationship! "The secret of the LORD is with those who fear Him, And He will show them His covenant" (Psalm 25:14). We find unlimited joy in time with the Lord, as He reveals what His covenant means in our day-to-day lives. We only share secrets with trusted friends. I want to be a trusted friend to God, so we can share secrets with each other.

## SECRETS REVEALED

We have a wonderful promise of intimacy in scripture. "I will give you the treasures of darkness and hidden riches of secret places, that you may know that I, the LORD, who call you by your name, am the God of Israel" (Isaiah 45:3). Not only does God call us by name, but He also will deliver to us the "treasures of darkness," or difficult truths about Himself which we will treasure, and the gift of the "riches of secret places," which represent the richness of the depths of His heart.

"He reveals deep and secret things; He knows what is in the darkness, and light dwells with Him" (Daniel 2:22). As we seek Him for answers from those areas of darkness or the unknown, He promises to shine His light of revelation upon them for us to see and understand. My heart has taken such comfort as I have read and woven these scriptural truths about Him into my faith and daily Christian life. God wishes to share with us so very much.

We can know beyond any doubt that He is faithful to His Word. God cannot and would not ever lie or deceive us as we pursue Him! Listen to what Jesus said in Matthew 13. "That it might be fulfilled which was spoken by the prophet, saying: 'I will open My mouth in parables; I will utter things kept secret from the foundation of the world'" (v. 35). One of Jesus' greatest blessings to those He taught was the ability to take powerful truths and place them in simple, everyday stories. In this way, none would miss what He was saying, even those things that had been unknown from the founding of the earth.

"For there is nothing hidden which will not be revealed, nor has anything been kept secret but that it should come to light" (Mark 4:22). We must examine this final scripture as Christ placed it, between two separate parables. Jesus had just finished explaining the parable of the sower to His disciples. He then brings out this word picture:

> Also He said to them, "Is a lamp brought to be put under a basket or under a bed? Is it not to be set on a lampstand? For there is nothing hidden which will not be revealed, nor has anything been kept secret but that it should come to light. If anyone has ears to hear, let him hear." Then He said to them, "Take heed what you hear. With the same measure you use, it will be measured to you; and to you who hear, more will be given. For whoever has, to him more will be given; but whoever does not have, even what he has will be taken away from him." (Mark 4:21–25)

Jesus is asking, "Do you take a light and place it in a place it isn't useful, or do you place it on a lampstand to take full advantage of the light?" The light represents the truth of revelation from God. We must use truth in our lives properly and effectively. Jesus is speaking about the light of revealed truth and its activity. Do not take truth and squander it by placing it on the shelf—put it to use.

## USE TRUTH CORRECTLY

Jesus's promise is that nothing will remain hidden from those who pursue God's truth, and all secrets are to "come to light" or to be revealed. The proper use of truth is to destroy falsehoods in all areas.

We are encouraged to use the truth we *hear,* and as we use that truth to transform our lives, God will give even greater truths to us. Out of this exchange, faith in God's Word is established and it transforms our belief system. (Remember that God's Word includes His speaking to our hearts, which is the revealed Word, not just the written Word.) Whoever has faith in God's Word, He will give them more truth to transform their life, according to Mark 4.

We can clearly see a foundation of truth, which brings enlightenment and transformation in our lives, in this scripture: "Whom will he teach knowledge? And whom will he make to understand the message? Those just weaned from milk? Those just drawn from the breasts? For precept must be upon precept, precept upon precept, line upon line, line upon line, here a little, there a little" (Isaiah 28:9–10).

Together these scriptures carry the promise from God to us that those things which we describe as secret, unknown, treasures of darkness, riches of secret places, deep or hidden, can be revealed to those who desire it. God says you can have this knowledge, but it only comes from Him through relationship.

In 2 Peter 1:3, Peter says that God called us by His own "glory and virtue" to have relationship, and out of this relationship, we would know what has been provided by God for us in the areas of both the necessities for life and godliness. Let me rephrase the verse this way for simplicity. "As His divine power has given to us all things that pertain to *life . . .*, through the knowledge of Him who called us by glory and virtue." God's unstoppable power pours out all we need for life because of our knowledge of Him.

## A Story of a Miracle

How does knowing God provide for your life? Remember that life is simply being alive or existing, both in our body and in our soul or spirit. With this truth in mind, let us apply this verse to real life by sharing a true story.

In 2006, my son, David, had a spontaneous pneumothorax (which is a sudden hole in the lung). On the way to the hospital, God shared specific events with me, which would occur as the day went on, and showed me what I was to do. Because I knew God's voice through time spent with Him, I knew to trust what He revealed to me.

After the doctors had examined David, I waited until they left the room and then did exactly what God had shown me in a vision to do. David was on the gurney in extreme pain and I just laid my hands upon him and felt the release of God's power, as I was obedient. I did not pray or even say a word. Immediately, I could see the response to God's touch on David's body as both his face and the tension in his body relaxed. According to David, his pain threshold went from ten down to about four in less than thirty seconds.

The rest of David's testimony is that not only was his miraculous healing completed in twenty-four hours, but a powerful spiritual download occurred at the same moment. David has never been the same since. His spiritual dimension has dramatically increased. So let me say that what the enemy worked for destruction was exchanged for God's glory and David's empowerment.

## Intimacy Brings Favor

As we previously discussed, we can look at life as a journey, or path. Paths come in every shape, size, and destination. King David said it like this, "You will show me the path of life; in Your presence is fullness of joy; at Your right hand are pleasures forevermore" (Psalm 16:11). As our relationship with God deepens and intimacy increases, so does the moment-to-moment direction of our lives by our beloved Lord. Because He holds our heart, we easily yield to His wooing and direction. As He carries us along life's path, we experience indescribable joy and pure pleasure.

Much like the Song of Solomon, the Beloved "takes our breath away." Just to be in His presence energizes our spirits, as well as our bodies. Life that flows from God Himself to us is just one aspect of what it means to be intimate with Him.

"I will never forget Your precepts, for by them You have given me life. I am Yours, save me; for I have sought Your precepts" (Psalm 119:93–94). The proclamation, "I am Yours," stirs my heart. Finding our life interwoven with God's precepts (or principles), His words, and His promised intimacy, fills us with His wisdom. Look at what wisdom says about itself—"For whoever finds me finds life, And obtains favor from the LORD" (Proverbs 8:35).

Favor from the Lord is a great gift that we must never squander. You gain momentum from knowing God's face and His pleasure are being directed toward you and your life, and that all of heaven is behind you. That momentum carries you through all the workings of destiny in your life.

Along with favor, the fear of the Lord holds great promise for a Christian. "The fear of the LORD leads to life, and he who has it will abide in satisfaction; He will not be visited with evil" (Proverbs 19:23). Those who have the fear of the Lord continually increasing in their lives will also have complete satisfaction. I am not describing the fear of retaliation from God, but the reverence of Him and His greatness. This is a place similar to what Psalms 91describes:

> He who dwells in the secret place of the Most High Shall abide under the shadow of the Almighty. I will say of the LORD, "He is my refuge and my fortress; my God, in Him I will trust." Surely He shall deliver you from the snare of the fowler and from the perilous pestilence.
>
> He shall cover you with His feathers, and under His wings you shall take refuge; His truth shall be your shield and buckler. You shall not be afraid of the terror by night, nor of the arrow that flies by day, nor of the pestilence that walks in darkness, nor of the destruction that lays waste at noonday. A thousand may fall at your side, and ten thousand at your right hand; but it shall not come near you.
>
> Only with your eyes shall you look, and see the reward of the wicked. Because you have made the LORD, who is my refuge, even the Most High, your dwelling place, no evil shall befall you, nor shall any plague come near your dwelling; for He shall give His angels charge over you, to keep you in all your ways. In their hands they shall bear you up, lest you dash your foot against a stone.
>
> You shall tread upon the lion and the cobra, the young lion and the serpent you shall trample underfoot. "Because he has set his love upon Me, therefore I will deliver him; I will set him on high, because he has known My name. He shall call upon Me, and I will answer him; I will be with him in trouble; I will deliver him and honor him. With long life I will satisfy him, and show him My salvation." (vv. 1–16)

Now that is what I call living! As for satisfaction, I believe this describes it perfectly. What more could we desire, than this type of *life?*

## HUMILITY

Humility works hand in hand with the fear of the Lord. "By humility and the fear of the LORD are riches and honor and life" (Proverbs 22:4). According to this scripture, in order to have riches, honor, and life, we need to have humility, as well as the fear of the Lord. A Christian builds the foundation of their life upon Christ first, and then humility and the fear of the Lord are building blocks laid by God as He fashions us.

Having humility placed in our life is similar to a grinding process. Pride must be ground away so as not to trip us and cause us to stumble. Humility, working hand-in-hand with the fear of the Lord, begins the building process of great character. Having great character enables us to hold true to ourselves, as well as to God. Shallow character allows weakness to be exploited, which plays into the hands of the enemy.

## WISDOM AND TRUTH

The failure of many of those in ministry is a constant reminder to all of us of how sly the enemy is to attack our weak areas. "For wisdom is a defense as money is a defense, but the excellence of knowledge is that wisdom gives life to those who have it" (Ecclesiastes 7:12). Here we understand what wisdom has the potential to do. Wisdom is a defense that, unlike money, cannot be lost or stolen. The excellent part is that wisdom gives life as well. I would rather have wisdom than anything else, because with wisdom I can access anything I need.

This is what *not* having Godly wisdom looks like:

This I say, therefore, and testify in the Lord, that you should no longer walk as the rest of the Gentiles walk, in the futility of their mind, having their understanding darkened, being alienated from the life of God, because of the ignorance that is in them, because of the blindness of their heart; who, being past feeling, have given themselves over to lewdness, to work all uncleanness with greediness. But you have not so learned Christ, if indeed you have heard Him and have been taught by Him, as the truth is in Jesus: that you put off, concerning your former conduct, the old man which grows corrupt according to the deceitful lusts, and be renewed in the spirit of your mind, and that you put on the new man which was created according to God, in true righteousness and holiness. (Ephesians 4:17–24)

Ignorance, blindness, and a hardened heart creates futility of the mind. This sickness darkens the understanding and separates the individual from the *life of God.* This sickened state also leads to ungodly lifestyles. As a Christian, we hear Jesus and He teaches us. Truth is the by-product of a relationship with Christ.

The renewing of the mind with truth breaks the connections with the "old man," so we are free to put on the "new man." The choice to follow-through rests on us individually. This process describes the concept of "revelation leads to salvation, which leads to sanctification." We walk in the Spirit from within the realm of the "new man." "There is therefore now no condemnation to those who are in Christ Jesus, who do not walk according to the flesh, but according to the Spirit" (Romans 8:1).

I say then: Walk in the Spirit, and you shall not fulfill the lust of the flesh. For the flesh lusts against the Spirit, and the Spirit against the flesh; and these are contrary to one another, so that you do not do the things that you wish. But if you are led by the Spirit, you are not under the law.

Now the works of the flesh are evident, which are: adultery, fornication, uncleanness, lewdness, idolatry, sorcery, hatred, contentions, jealousies, outbursts of wrath, selfish ambitions, dissensions, heresies, envy, murders, drunkenness, revelries, and the like; of which I tell you beforehand, just as I also told *you* in time past, that those who practice such things will not inherit the kingdom of God.

But the fruit of the Spirit is love, joy, peace, longsuffering, kindness, goodness, faithfulness, gentleness, self-control. Against such there is no law. And those *who are* Christ's have crucified the flesh with its passions and desires. If we live in the Spirit, let us also walk in the Spirit. (Galatians 5:16–25)

The transformation from "old" to "new" man and "walking in the Spirit" all refer to a journey. Just like when we choose to take a walk, this journey is a choice. We choose to start it, we choose to continue along the path, and we can choose at any point to stop. However, when we see how the Lord provides for us as we go along, and what blessings come our way along the path and the reward that awaits us at the end, there is no valid reason to stop that cannot be overcome by the goodness of the Lord.

We never face the challenges in life alone. "I have been crucified with Christ; it is no longer I who live, but Christ lives in me; and the life which I now live in the flesh I live by faith in the Son of

God, who loved me and gave Himself for me" (Galatians 2:20). As Galatians 5 encourages us to crucify the flesh, it is in Galatians 2 that we see the beauty of being "crucified with Christ," of having a life where Christ lives within us, thus allowing us to live that life by faith, knowing that Jesus will enable, as well as empower, us to live in a godly manner.

## ABUNDANT LIFE

Living in this manner delivers wave upon wave of joy. "You have made known to me the ways of life; You will make me full of joy in Your presence" (Acts 2:28). As Christ lives through the believer, we learn the ways of His life and with Him directing our steps. Within His presence, we experience heavenly joy. Jesus describes this overcoming life in John 10. "The thief does not come except to steal, and to kill, and to destroy. I have come that they may have life, and that they may have it more abundantly" (v. 10). There is no other way to find this "life more abundant" than through Christ Himself.

Where does this life come from? "For as the Father has life in Himself, so He has granted the Son to have life in Himself" (John 5:26). All life comes from the Father. It is not randomly reproduced or created, but the Father speaks it into existence at His command. God the Father placed life from Himself into Jesus, and because Christ is our Savior, He deposits that same life into us.

There is no better way to glorify God than to live this style of life and share it with others. We reap the benefits of living for God. We do not lose anything, but we gain all things in Christ when we give ourselves to Him. John describes this life found within Christ. "In the beginning was the Word, and the Word was with God, and the Word was God. He was in the beginning with God. All things were made through Him, and without Him nothing was made that was made. In Him was life, and the life was the light of men" (John 1:1–4). This same light, or life, can be living in us as well. We must share this light and life with those lost in darkness.

## BASIC NEEDS

When we discuss life in terms of the basic needs to survive, we must first look at what Jesus said in Luke 12:

> Then He said to His disciples, "Therefore I say to you, do not worry about your life, what you will eat; nor about the body, what you will put on. Life is more than food, and the body is more than clothing." (vv. 22–23)

> And He said to them, "Take heed and beware of covetousness, for one's life does not consist in the abundance of the things he possesses." (v. 15)

This way of thinking runs contrary to what many people believe is true. Happiness never comes from our belongings. Our possessions must never possess us. When we are possessed by our possessions, we can fall prey to the challenges of life similar to those Jesus describes in Luke 8. "Now the ones that fell among thorns are those who, when they have heard, go out and are choked with cares, riches, and pleasures of life, and bring no fruit to maturity" (v. 14). The discouragement experienced by those pictured here gives little encouragement to those who witness their downfall.

Jesus has much to say about life:

> Therefore I say to you, do not worry about your life, what you will eat or what you will drink; nor about your body,

what you will put on. Is not life more than food and the body more than clothing? Look at the birds of the air, for they neither sow nor reap nor gather into barns; yet your heavenly Father feeds them. Are you not of more value than they?

Which of you by worrying can add one cubit to his stature? So why do you worry about clothing? Consider the lilies of the field, how they grow: they neither toil nor spin; and yet I say to you that even Solomon in all his glory was not arrayed like one of these.

Now if God so clothes the grass of the field, which today is, and tomorrow is thrown into the oven, will He not much more clothe you, O you of little faith? Therefore do not worry, saying, "What shall we eat?" or "What shall we drink?" or "What shall we wear?" For after all these things the Gentiles seek. For your heavenly Father knows that you need all these things.

But seek first the kingdom of God and His righteousness, and all these things shall be added to you. Therefore do not worry about tomorrow, for tomorrow will worry about its own things. Sufficient for the day is its own trouble. (Matthew 6:25–34)

"All these things" that "will be added" to you in verse 33 are the essentials of life. As we are joined with the Kingdom of God, as well as His righteousness, our focus is moved from ourselves and placed back upon the true needs of life, which are the Kingdom and the King. The King provides for us from His table. Our relationship and inheritance guarantees provision for the necessities of life from God's hand. We can preach this universal truth on every continent in the world.

Jesus is a real encouragement to us when He says in Luke, "Do not fear, little flock, for it is your Father's good pleasure to give you the kingdom" (Luke 12:32). Jesus knew how heavily the concerns of daily needs would weigh upon us. I hear great compassion in His tone—"Don't fear *little flock.*" The exhortation that our Father finds great pleasure in giving us His kingdom, sparks hope in times of great distress.

I may sound repetitious about how God feels toward us, but I have found that it can be easier to believe the bad than the good. I also believe repetition is good for establishing new truths in a belief system. How does your belief system stand up to the promises of God?

## KNOW THE WORD

It is important to meditate on the Word of God. Jesus said something profound in John 6 about the Holy Spirit and His Word. "It is the Spirit who gives life; the flesh profits nothing. The words that I speak to you are spirit, and they are life" (v. 63). Meditating on and repeating the Word of God causes a transformation to occur.

Look at Matthew 8, where the centurion felt unworthy to have Jesus under his roof. He asked Jesus just to speak the word and he knew his servant would be healed, in verses 5–13. Jesus's Word carries creative power and we should learn to handle it wisely. "Be diligent to present yourself approved to God, a worker who does not need to be ashamed, rightly dividing the word of truth" (2 Timothy 2:15).

It takes times of study to learn to use the Word properly. As the Word of God becomes a part of our life, we make changes in our lifestyle, which others will notice. The Word of God will be the basis of our life. Defined study of the Word, using a method that works best for you, will replace "biblical Russian roulette," where you randomly open the Bible and point to find answers for the day.

Finally, let us look at what Jesus said about Himself in John 11 and 14.

> Jesus said to her, "I am the resurrection and the life. He who believes in Me, though he may die, he shall live. And whoever lives and believes in Me shall never die. Do you believe this?" (11:25–26)

> Jesus said to him, "I am the way, the truth, and the life. No one comes to the Father except through Me." (14:6)

Together these scriptures paint a powerful picture of an awesome Savior's promise to us. Jesus is the *resurrection* life. He is *life* in all its glory. He is the *way* to life, the *truth,* and the only way to the Father. With all of these incredible proclamations of Himself, we need Him in our lives. "He who finds his life will lose it, and he who loses his life for My sake will find it" (Matthew 10:39). If you are seeking life, you will only find it in Him. Attempting to find satisfaction anywhere else will cause you to lose your life, according to that verse, so why waste your energy and gamble your eternal soul on anyone else.

I will closer this chapter with this verse. "Blessed is the man who endures temptation; for when he has been approved, he will receive the crown of life which the Lord has promised to those who love Him" (James 1:12).

# . . . And Godliness

For God knows that in the day you eat of it your eyes will be opened, and you will be like God, knowing good and evil. (Genesis 3:5)

"You will be like God..." Satan, in the form of the serpent, was true to his character as he twisted God's Word to Eve. So began the pursuit of being like God.

## Being Like God

I believe that God intended for humanity to be like Him, so being *like God* is not out of the question for us as Christians. "Then God said, 'Let Us make man in Our image, according to Our likeness; let them have dominion over the fish of the sea, over the birds of the air, and over the cattle, over all the earth and over every creeping thing that creeps on the earth'" (Genesis 1:26). Being made in God's "likeness" has many aspects, one of which is the ability to have dominion or authority. God has the ultimate dominion over all things, so similarly, He made us in His likeness, and gave us dominion over the earth. We need His guidance in fulfilling the responsibility that accompanies this great blessing.

Adam had an intimate relationship with God as they walked in the garden, which God used to mold Adam for his role of dominant ruler upon the earth. God mentored Adam through the many hours spent with Him.

> Out of the ground the LORD God formed every beast of the field and every bird of the air, and brought them to Adam to see what he would call them. And whatever Adam called each living creature, that was its name. So Adam gave names to all cattle, to the birds of the air, and to every beast of the field. But for Adam there was not found a helper comparable to him. (Genesis 2:19–20)

Have you ever thought about this moment in history? Adam and God, side by side, as He brought each creature out before Adam and said, "Well, Adam, what do you think we should call this one?" What a heart-touching moment of a Father and His son (creation). Imagine the hours spent together, and the joy that God must have experienced as He watched Adam's face as he saw creatures and mulled over what to name them. As a father, I have experienced this type of joy with my own children.

This is only one glimpse into God and Adam's relationship, but I hope you see how being like God was in God's heart for humanity from the beginning. We tend to be like those we spend time with, and I believe that as Adam spent time with God, he started to take on attributes of Him. If we wish to be godly, we should make it our goal to spend time with Him. Let God rub off on you and see how you are changed.

## BEING GODLY

*Webster's New World Dictionary* defines "godly" as, "of or from God; divine and also devoted to God; pious; devout; religious—godliness[16]." *Vine's Expository Dictionary of Old and New Testament Words* gives this explanation of the Greek word εὐσέβεια, translated "eusebeia," (Strong's Number G2150): "from *eu*, 'well,' and *sebomai*, 'to be devout,' denotes that piety which, characterized by a Godward attitude, does that which is well-pleasing to Him[17]."

"As His divine power has given to us all things that pertain to life and godliness, through the knowledge of Him who called us by glory and virtue" (2 Peter 1:3). Peter is saying here that God calls us by His own "glory and virtue" to have relationship, and out of this relationship we will know what has been provided by God for us in the arena of godliness, as well as life. God's unstoppable power pours forth all we need for godliness in this life because of our knowledge of Him. A godly attitude finds fulfillment in doing all that pleases God, thus brings godliness.

> But if I am delayed, I write so that you may know how you ought to conduct yourself in the house of God, which is the church of the living God, the pillar and ground of the truth. And without controversy great is the mystery of godliness: God was manifested in the flesh, justified in the Spirit, seen by angels, preached among the Gentiles, believed on in the world, received up in glory. (1 Timothy 3:15–16)

Just as Christ walked in godliness, so must we. We must conduct ourselves in such a way as not to bring shame to or discredit the kingdom of God, to the best of our abilities. God's continuing work in our lives will enable us to walk in higher levels of godliness, if we will hold fast to Him.

## PRAY FOR YOUR LEADERS

Timothy has much to say on the subject of godliness: "Therefore I exhort first of all that supplications, prayers, intercessions, and giving of thanks be made for all men, for kings and all who are in authority, that we may lead a quiet and peaceable life in all godliness and reverence" (1 Timothy 2:1–2). I believe that the prayer of intercession for those leaders who have oversight over you may contribute to the atmosphere of favor and blessings upon your life.

> And we urge you, brethren, to recognize those who labor among you, and are over you in the Lord and admonish you, and to esteem them very highly in love for their work's sake. Be at peace among yourselves. Now we exhort you, brethren, warn those who are unruly, comfort the fainthearted, uphold the weak, be patient with all. See that no one renders evil for evil to anyone, but always pursue what is good both for yourselves and for all. Rejoice always, pray without ceasing, in everything give thanks; for this is the will of God in Christ Jesus for you. Do not quench the Spirit. Do not despise prophecies. Test all things; hold fast what is good. Abstain from every form of evil. Now may the God of peace Himself sanctify you completely; and may your whole spirit, soul, and body be preserved blameless at the coming of our Lord Jesus

Christ. He who calls you is faithful, who also will do it. Brethren, pray for us. (1 Thessalonians 5:12–25)

The attributes of godliness found written here are an exhortation for all Christians to pursue and adhere to. As a leader, I feel very strongly about Christians esteeming their leaders highly with love because of the responsibility the leaders carry. I ask that you pray for us leaders to clearly hear the Word of the Lord and boldly proclaim it. 1 Timothy 4 gives the reason I ask for this type of prayer:

If you instruct the brethren in these things, you will be a good minister of Jesus Christ, nourished in the words of faith and of the good doctrine which you have carefully followed. But reject profane and old wives' fables, and exercise yourself toward godliness. For bodily exercise profits a little, but godliness is profitable for all things, having promise of the life that now is and of that which is to come. (vv. 6–8)

I believe every leader wants to be their best for the sake of the Kingdom. With that in mind, the actions of a leader should be to nourish others out of the abundance of "good doctrine," as well as "the words of faith." The challenge to "exercise . . . toward godliness" will be different depending upon the individual leader, but the overall target will remain the same—that of Christ-likeness.

## BLESSINGS ARE NOW

I do not want to miss this statement: "but godliness is profitable for all things, having promise of the life that now is and of that which is to come." This point is vitally important: "promise of the life that *now is and of that which is to come.*" I want to stress the point that we do not have to wait for the blessings of godliness until we reach heaven, but can partake of them here and now in this life and time. Yes, godliness awaits us in the eternal, but as God calls us to walk as Christ walked, wouldn't levels of godliness on this side of heaven be helpful in living life more abundantly as Christ proclaimed we could?

"For He says: 'In an acceptable time I have heard you, and in the day of salvation I have helped you.' Behold, *now* is the accepted time; behold, *now* is the day of salvation" (2 Corinthians 6:2). *Now* is the day of the favor of the Lord, and every day new levels of understanding of our salvation brings us into deeper levels of godliness. Remember Webster's definition of godliness as being "of or from God and or divine." The existence of godliness in one's life is a tribute to the inward change that has or is occurring as the Lord influences a life.

As we have a continuing relationship with God, His divine influence rubs off on us. What we focus on is what we become. If you focus on the attributes of holiness as you interact with God, you will take on some of His attributes intrinsically. Most of all, remember, "godliness is profitable for all things."

## PURSUIT OF GODLINESS

"Now godliness with contentment is great gain. For we brought nothing into this world, and it is certain we can carry nothing out. And having food and clothing, with these we shall be content" (1 Timothy 6:6–8). The partnership of "having all things pertaining to life and godliness" brings us into a fulfilling environment where the increase of God's kingdom is limitless and unending.

The downfall of many is the love of the riches, replacing the love of God. Timothy is encouraged to flee from such distractions. "But you, O man of God, flee these things and pursue righteousness, godliness, faith, love, patience, gentleness" (1 Timothy 6:11). The best part of this type of pursuit is knowing who is running alongside of you as you go. The Holy Spirit guides us in our pursuits of godliness and the knowledge of God.

Along with all the "things pertaining to life and godliness," His glory and virtue also carry "exceedingly great and precious promises," which are the doorway to being a "partaker of His divine nature." "By which have been given to us exceedingly great and precious promises, that through these you may be partakers of the divine nature, having escaped the corruption that is in the world through lust" (2 Peter 1:4). These promises are always confirming our inheritance as children of God. "Whoever has been born of God does not sin, for His seed remains in him; and he cannot sin, because he has been born of God" (1 John 3:9). A partaker is someone who is "a companion, partner or has communion, or fellowship with another[18]."

Humanity lost its image of God when Adam and Eve fell, and inherited an un-godly image in its place. The escape from the corruption brought upon the earth at the fall has been, and will continue to be, the goal of the work of Christ. The conception of sin came from the lust of the flesh, but as we take on the nature of God, godliness is conceived within us. Sin is starved out and sanctification occurs under the graceful hand of God.

Because of the investment of God's glory and virtue, as well as the "great and precious promises" that accompany them, and the fact we have everything "pertaining to life and godliness," our response is pursuit. This type of pursuit is one of deep, earnest, all encompassing, pushing through all obstacles, never tiring pursuit.

You dream in your dreams about the pursuit. It is so real, you cannot imagine your life without it.

## ATTRIBUTES OF GODLINESS

The goal of this pursuit is the addition of virtue to your faith, and knowledge to your virtue. To knowledge, we are encouraged to add self-control, and to self-control, we add perseverance. These are to be incorporated with godliness, brotherly kindness, and love, according to 2 Peter 1:5–7.

As individuals, we must master these attributes. This is not like going to a store and placing each item into your cart. This is more like the mindset found in Luke 14:

For which of you, intending to build a tower, does not sit down first and count the cost, whether he has enough to finish it—lest, after he has laid the foundation, and is not able to finish, all who see it begin to mock him, saying, "This man began to build and was not able to finish." Or what king, going to make war against another king, does not sit down first and consider whether he is able with ten thousand to meet him who comes against him with twenty thousand? Or else, while the other is still a great way off, he sends a delegation and asks conditions of peace. So likewise, whoever of you does not forsake all that he has cannot be My disciple. (vv. 28–33)

The cost of this lifestyle may be more than some wish to pay, but if they truly examine the benefits of the sacrifice, I believe they will choose the way of Christ.

## BARREN VS. BIRTH

"For if these things are yours and abound, you will be neither barren nor unfruitful in the knowledge of our Lord Jesus Christ" (2 Peter 1:8). This scripture is so full of promise for those who have paid the price and flourish in the qualities mentioned above. As we increase in each of the attributes, we remove the impact of being barren and unfruitful in the knowledge of God.

What is it to be barren in the knowledge of the Lord? Barren, according to Webster, means "that cannot produce offspring; sterile, not bearing or pregnant at the regular time; said of animals or plants[19]." The Greek word for barren in this verse means idle or inactive.[20] If someone is barren of knowledge, it means the person is ignorant or lacks knowledge, not that the knowledge is unobtainable. When someone is barren, or lacking, in the knowledge of Jesus, there is a potential of gaining that knowledge through pursuit of Him.

Barren also speaks of the lack of birthing or new life. "Jesus said to him, 'I am the way, the truth, and the life. No one comes to the Father except through Me'" (John 14:6). This "life" is required to have barrenness broken off our lives. At one time, people considered a barren woman as cursed by God. With an intimate relationship with Christ, the curse is broken and we become impregnated (no longer barren) with the living knowledge of God.

"Therefore, my brethren, you also have become dead to the law through the body of Christ, that you may be married to another—to Him who was raised from the dead, that we should bear fruit to God" (Romans 7:4). This marriage to Christ produces life and fruitfulness. This enables new birth to occur in our own lives, as well as the ability to birth others into the kingdom of God through our testimony of Christ. This is the main idea of the Great Commission.

And He said to them, "Go into all the world and preach the gospel to every creature. He who believes and is baptized will be saved; but he who does not believe will be condemned. And these signs will follow those who believe: In My name they will cast out demons; they will speak with new tongues; they will take up serpents; and if they drink anything deadly, it will by no means hurt them; they will lay hands on the sick, and they will recover." (Mark 16:15–18)

"For whom He foreknew, He also predestined to be conformed to the image of His Son, that He might be the firstborn among many brethren. Moreover whom He predestined, these He also called; whom He called, these He also justified; and whom He justified, these He also glorified." (Romans 8: 29–30)

Reproduction in the kingdom takes on an entirely different angle when we see how God assists with signs and wonders. Matthew writes it this way:

And Jesus came and spoke to them, saying, "All authority has been given to Me in heaven and on earth. Go therefore and make disciples of all the nations, baptizing them in the name of the Father and of the Son and of the Holy Spirit, teaching them to observe all things that I have commanded you; and lo, I am with you always, even to the end of the age." Amen. (Matthew 28:18–20)

Just as we are to be "conformed into the likeness of Christ," which is to become more like Him each day, we also shall bring others into the kingdom as we work with God.

## HE FEEDS US

Webster defines "unfruitful" as "not reproducing; barren; unproductive, yielding no worthwhile results; fruitless; unprofitable[21]." We can look at this unfruitfulness as lacking hunger for spiritual food. This is similar to what Jesus spoke of in John 4: "But He said to them, 'I have food to eat of which you do not know.' Therefore the disciples said to one another, 'Has anyone brought Him anything to eat?' Jesus said to them, 'My food is to do the will of Him who sent Me, and to finish His work'" (John 4:32–34).

The satisfaction we find in doing the Father's will is indescribable. When you walk out the call of God that He has placed on your life, it places you in the center of God's blessings and provisions. "So He humbled you, allowed you to hunger, and fed you with manna which you did not know nor did your fathers know, that He might make you know that man shall not live by bread alone; but man lives by every word that proceeds from the mouth of the LORD" (Deuteronomy 8:3). Every word from God's lips is a delicious morsel for us to feast upon in the journey.

As we grow in maturity in Christ, God gives us deeper and deeper revelations of Himself, thus rooting us deeper in His truths.

> Moreover, brethren, I do not want you to be unaware that all our fathers were under the cloud, all passed through the sea, all were baptized into Moses in the cloud and in the sea, all ate the same spiritual food, and all drank the same spiritual drink. For they drank of that spiritual Rock that

followed them, and that Rock was Christ. (1 Corinthians 10:1–4)

We are under the cloud of God's protection and provision in our lives. The baptism we experience is of the Holy Spirit, as seen in Acts 11:15–16. The food and drink we have is the body and blood of Christ, according to Matthew 26:26–28 and John 6:53–56. Jesus is the rock that we build our lives on.

The fruit (or results) of revelation in our lives nourishes our spiritual walk and brings truth to us, which breaks the chains of bondage to ungodly living. We live by every word of revelation from God.

## TRUTH OR BLINDNESS?

Jesus often spoke of those who had eyes to see and ears to hear such as in Mark 8:18; Matthew 11:15, 13:9, 43, etc. As we listen to hear the Word of truth from Christ, we learn that He is trustworthy. "You also trusted, after you heard the word of truth, the gospel of your salvation; in whom also, having believed, you were sealed with the Holy Spirit of promise" (Ephesians 1:13). Salvation manifests each time truth enters our heart. God is continually taking territory within our lives as His truth renews our minds.

"And do not be conformed to this world, but be transformed by the renewing of your mind, that you may prove what is that good and acceptable and perfect will of God" (Romans 12:2). This "proving" is done as we live our lives before others. His Word reveals "the good and acceptable and perfect will of God" to us as we receive the fresh Word of God every day.

For those who choose not to pursue the attributes of faith—virtue, knowledge, self-control, perseverance, godliness, brotherly kindness, and love—Peter declares them "shortsighted, even to blindness" (2 Peter 1:9). This blindness causes them to forget that they were "cleansed from their old sin." How sad to fall into this devastation of forgetfulness. Blindness to spiritual realities causes many to stumble and fall from grace, even going so far as to forget how marvelous salvation was.

Once these steps have begun, few have been able to retrace them back to refresh their salvation. Most often, the forgetfulness progresses from simply losing the truth of who we are in Christ, into a full-blown hardened heart. In this state, doubt creeps in and smothers all memories of the goodness of God. The next step is the questioning of whether anything that the person once believed was actually true or just zeal and emotion. The final state is the full rejection of Christ and salvation as mere emotionalism.

Our exhortation is found in the following verse: "Therefore, brethren, be even more diligent to make your call and election sure, for if you do these things you will never stumble" (2 Peter 1:10). The effort used to establish both the election and call comes from drawing upon God's strength. We must do our part and God does His. We first receive the call and the election follows. Romans 8 makes this clear:

> And we know that all things work together for good to those who love God, to those who are the called according to His purpose. For whom He foreknew, He also predestined to be conformed to the image of His Son, that He might be the firstborn among many brethren. Moreover whom He predestined, these He also called; whom He called, these He also justified; and whom He justified, these He also glorified. What then shall we say to these things? If God is for us, who can be against us? He who did not spare His own Son, but delivered Him up for us all,

how shall He not with Him also freely give us all things? Who shall bring a charge against God's elect? It is God who justifies. (Romans 8:28–33)

Here we see how the call eventually leads to being one of the "elect." As we are diligent to follow God's lead, we mature to the level of not stumbling or failing.

## THE REWARDS OF PURSUIT

Those who have persevered to this point of growth experience an open heaven. "For so an entrance will be supplied to you abundantly into the everlasting kingdom of our Lord and Savior Jesus Christ" (2 Peter 1:11). I believe that as we pursue God in all the avenues described here, we have the potential of Him rewarding us with an open heaven here and now, much like what God describes in Malachi 3. "'Bring all the tithes into the storehouse, that there may be food in My house, and try Me now in this,' Says the LORD of hosts, 'If I will not open for you the windows of heaven and pour out for you such blessing that there will not be room enough to receive it'" (Malachi 3:10).

Our obedience in pursuit will bring indescribable rewards. "But without faith it is impossible to please Him, for he who comes to God must believe that He is, and that He is a rewarder of those who diligently seek Him" (Hebrews 11:6).

Jesus confidently states in several instances about where He had come from:

Not that anyone has seen the Father, except *He who is from God;* He has seen the Father. (John 6:46)

Jesus said to them, "If God were your Father, you would love Me, for *I proceeded forth and came from God;* nor have I come of Myself, but He sent Me." (John 8:42)

For the Father Himself loves you, because you have loved Me, and have believed that *I came forth from God.* I came forth from the Father and have come into the world. Again, I leave the world and go to the Father. (John 16:27–28)

Jesus knew fully who He was, what He was to do, and where He was going. No one detoured Him from that path. His self-confidence was obvious to all, even those opposed to His message. Finally, in John 13 we see the full purpose of a life fully lived for the Kingdom. "Jesus, knowing that the Father had given all things into His hands, and that He had come from God and was going to God, rose from supper and laid aside His garments, took a towel and girded Himself" (vv. 3–4).

The understanding of the truth that Christ had about His identity in that moment should get your attention. Jesus knew that "the Father had given all things into His hands." That statement echoes of what we read in 2 Peter 1:3: "As His divine power has given to us *all things* that pertain to life and godliness, through the knowledge of Him who called us by glory and virtue." From the Father's "glory and virtue," He has given us all things, just like Jesus. The question that we need to answer is, "What do I do with it?"

Jesus, with His knowledge of what was going to happen to Him, rose from the place of supper and "laid aside His garments." This speaks of leaving the place of rest and refreshing, and setting aside His divinity to do an act of servant-hood by washing the disciples' feet. He gave us this perfect example of servitude to follow.

Even though we have "everything pertaining to life and godliness," we are to use it to bring glory to the King and His Kingdom.

> For I consider that the sufferings of this present time are not worthy to be compared with the glory which shall be revealed in us. For the earnest expectation of the creation eagerly waits for the revealing of the sons of God. For the creation was subjected to futility, not willingly, but because of Him who subjected it in hope; because the creation itself also will be delivered from the bondage of corruption into the glorious liberty of the children of God. For we know that the whole creation groans and labors with birth pangs together until now. (Romans 8:18–22)

Pursuing "the knowledge of Him who called us by glory and virtue" results in our "revealing" as "the sons of God." The entire world will be "delivered" into the "glorious liberty of the children of God" from its current "corruption."

## THE "I AM"

We carry the seed of God, as well as the seeds of the Kingdom, within us. When Moses asked for God's name in Exodus 3:14, the response was "I am who I am." John says:

> Jesus therefore, knowing all things that would come upon Him, went forward and said to them, "Whom are you seeking?" They answered Him, "Jesus of Nazareth." Jesus said to them, *"I am He."* And Judas, who betrayed Him,

also stood with them. Now when He said to them, "I am He," they drew back and fell to the ground. (John 18:4–6)

But by the grace of God *I am what I am*, and His grace toward me was not in vain; but I labored more abundantly than they all, yet not I, but the grace of God which was with me. (1 Corinthians 15:10)

The references in these scriptures to "I am" show you something of the divine influence in God's children. Just as a son carries his father's family name, I believe Jesus, in His response, proclaimed His greatness and lineage as He said, "I am."

I also believe the same can be applied to the apostle Paul when he exclaimed, "I am what I am" because of God's grace. The most significant part of this grace is that it was not given "in vain." Paul responded to the grace by being diligent to co-labor with it and the Spirit to establish great change in his life.

We also carry the divine influence of the great "I am" within our spirit. As we walk in the godliness provided by God, allow the greatness of the "I am" to initiate godly change within you.

## Do Not Try, Just Be

"Therefore purge out the old leaven, that you may be a new lump, since you truly are unleavened. For indeed Christ, our Passover, was sacrificed for us" (1 Corinthians 5:7). I have a favorite saying, which goes like this: "Stop trying to be a Christian and just be one." Paul exhorted the Corinthians to be a *new lump* by purging out the old leaven, but he added that they already were unleavened. Paul was saying that Christ as the Passover had removed the leaven and made them unleavened, even though the manifestation of what Christ had done was not evident in their lives.

I base my saying on a similar concept. I believe that since I am seated with Christ in the heavenly places, according to Ephesians 2:6, as a new creation, in a place of authority and wholeness, I can walk closely to Christ-likeness because of the finished work within me. I walk within the truth that I no longer need to try to be anything, because it is "Christ in me, the hope of glory" (Colossians 1:27), which transforms me into the likeness of Him. There is no room for striving or wrestling because my "old man" is dead and I am alive to Christ. "I have been crucified with Christ; it is no longer I who live, but Christ lives in me; and the life which I now live in the flesh I live by faith in the Son of God, who loved me and gave Himself for me" (Galatians 2:20). Therefore, I encourage you to stop trying to be, and just be.

> However, we speak wisdom among those who are mature, yet not the wisdom of this age, nor of the rulers of this age, who are coming to nothing. But we speak the wisdom of God in a mystery, the hidden wisdom which God ordained before the ages for our glory, which none of the rulers of this age knew; for had they known, they would not have crucified the Lord of glory. But as it is written:
>
> "Eye has not seen, nor ear heard, nor have entered into the heart of man the things which God has prepared for those who love Him."
>
> But God has revealed them to us through His Spirit. For the Spirit searches all things, yes, the deep things of God. For what man knows the things of a man except the spirit of the man which is in him? Even so no one knows the things of God except the Spirit of God. Now we have

received, not the spirit of the world, but the Spirit who is from God, that we might know the things that have been freely given to us by God.

These things we also speak, not in words which man's wisdom teaches but which the Holy Spirit teaches, comparing spiritual things with spiritual. But the natural man does not receive the things of the Spirit of God, for they are foolishness to him; nor can he know them, because they are spiritually discerned. But he who is spiritual judges all things, yet he himself is rightly judged by no one. For "who has known the mind of the LORD that he may instruct Him?" But we have the mind of Christ. (1 Corinthians 2:6–16)

The Spirit will reveal all the knowledge that we need to have access to life and godliness. I know this to be a true and trustworthy promise from God. "Now we have received, not the spirit of the world, but the Spirit who is from God, that we might know the things that have *been freely given to us by God*" (1 Corinthians 2:12).

If while reading this book you found only one usable truth, I pray that it is that this understanding transforms your life as you grow in the knowledge of Him. The change of your life, even in the slightest way, achieves the purpose that God gave me to write this book. May your prayer be that the Father completes all His desires and purposes in your life. Praise the Lord.

# How To Be Saved

So they said, "Believe on the Lord Jesus Christ, and you will be saved, you and your household." (Acts 16:31)

For "whoever calls on the name of the LORD shall be saved." (Romans 10:13)

To "believe on the Lord Jesus Christ" means to believe that Jesus is God's only Son, and that He is the Savior of all humanity.

For God so loved the world that He gave His only begotten Son, that whoever believes in Him should not perish but have everlasting life. (John 3:16)

Sin has separated us from God for eternity, but Jesus took our sin upon Himself when He died on the cross, which made a way for us to be reconciled to God and to spend eternity with Him in heaven.

> For the wages of sin is death, but the gift of God is eternal life in Christ Jesus our Lord. (Romans 6:23)

> For there is one God and one Mediator between God and men, the Man Christ Jesus, who gave Himself a ransom for all, to be testified in due time. (1 Timothy 2:5–6)

> And this is the testimony: that God has given us eternal life, and this life is in His Son. (1 John 5:11)

> He who believes in the Son has everlasting life; and he who does not believe the Son shall not see life, but the wrath of God abides on him. (John 3:36)

To be free from sin, we must acknowledge that we are sinners and that the only way to be free of sin is through Jesus, by accepting Him as our Savior.

> That if you confess with your mouth the Lord Jesus and believe in your heart that God has raised Him from the dead, you will be saved. For with the heart one believes unto righteousness, and with the mouth confession is made unto salvation. (Romans 10:9–10)

Jesus is the only way to God. No other religion or religious leader will get you to heaven.

Jesus said to him, "I am the way, the truth, and the life. No one comes to the Father except through Me." (John 14:6)

He who has the Son has life; he who does not have the Son of God does not have life. (1 John 5:12)

We must also understand that after dying on the cross for us, Jesus conquered death and was resurrected, and is alive today, sitting at God's right hand, praying for us.

. . . It is Christ who died, and furthermore is also risen, who is even at the right hand of God, who also makes intercession for us. (Romans 8:34)

Jesus did not leave us here on this earth alone. He sent His Holy Spirit to earth, to live inside of us, to become one with our spirit.

And I will pray the Father, and He will give you another Helper, that He may abide with you forever—the Spirit of truth, whom the world cannot receive, because it neither sees Him nor knows Him; but you know Him, for He dwells with you and will be in you. (John 14:16–17)

But the Helper, the Holy Spirit, whom the Father will send in My name, He will teach you all things, and bring to your remembrance all things that I said to you. (John 14:26)

Nevertheless I tell you the truth. It is to your advantage that I go away; for if I do not go away, the Helper will not come to you; but if I depart, I will send Him to you. And when He has come, He will convict the world of sin, and of righteousness, and of judgment: of sin, because they do not believe in Me; of righteousness, because I go to My Father and you see Me no more; of judgment, because the ruler of this world is judged. I still have many things to say to you, but you cannot bear them now. However, when He, the Spirit of truth, has come, He will guide you into all truth; for He will not speak on His own authority, but whatever He hears He will speak; and He will tell you things to come. He will glorify Me, for He will take of what is Mine and declare it to you. All things that the Father has are Mine. Therefore I said that He will take of Mine and declare it to you. (John 16:7–15)

If you are ready to be saved, say this prayer: "Dear Jesus, I admit that I am a sinner, that I have done and said many things not pleasing to You. Please forgive me of my sins. Wash my heart clean of all evil thoughts and intentions. Come into my heart and my life and be my Lord and Savior.

"Holy Spirit, I ask You to come into me right now, and fill me up. Replace my ungodly ways with Your ways. Teach me how to live my life in a way that is pleasing to You. Open my ears to hear Your voice and speak to my heart. Teach me how to obey You. Fill me with Your love, and teach me how to love others, as You love me.

"Help me grow in my relationship with You. Show me what church to go to that will help me grow in my Christian walk, and give me godly friends that will be an encouragement to me when I am having difficulties.

"Jesus, thank You for saving me. I love You.

"In Jesus' name I pray, Amen."

Romans 10:9 tells us that we must "confess with our mouth"—go and tell someone what you have just done. Find a local church to fellowship in, and talk to Jesus. He loves you and wants to talk to you.

Lastly, get a Bible if you do not already have one, preferably an easy-to-read translation, like the New International Version, and begin to read it. A good place to start is in the New Testament, which is in the latter part of the Bible, and read the book of John, which tells you the story of Jesus. Then continue reading from there.

Welcome to the family of God!

# NOTES

Chapter 1—Setting The Stage

[1] James Strong, *Strong's Talking Greek & Hebrew Dictionary,* (Austin, TX: WORD*search* Corp., 2007), WORD*search* CROSS e—book, s.v. "4690".

Chapter 2—My Responsibility

[2] Strong, *Strong's Talking,* s.v. "5281".

[3] Ibid., s.v. "2932".

[4] *Roget's International Thesaurus,* 4th ed., 761.15.

[5] Ibid., 808.2

[6] Strong, *Strong's Talking,* s.v. "5590".

[7] Tim Allen, *Galaxy Quest,* directed by Dean Parisot (Universal City, CA: DreamWorks Pictures, 1999), DVD.

Chapter 3—The Law is Weak

[8] Strong, *Strong's Talking,* s.v. "2937."

Chapter 4—God's Ways vs. His Acts

[9] John Ogilvie, *The Imperial Dictionary of the English Language: A Complete Encyclopedic Lexicon, Literary, Scientific, and Technological,* (Harvard University: Blackie & Son, 1883), vol. 3, s.v. "relationship."

Chapter 5—What Does a Journey Look Like?

[10] Laurence Fishburne and Keanu Reeves, "Rooftop Rescue," *The Matrix,* directed by Andy and Larry Wachowski (Burbank, CA: Warner Home Video, 1999), DVD.

Chapter 6—Of Life . . .

[11] *Webster's New World Dictionary of the American Language,* 2nd college ed., s.v. "life."

[12] *Roget's International Thesaurus,* 1.1.

[13] "Evan Roberts (minister)", website of Absolute Astronomy, accessed August 13, 2011, http://www.absolute-astronomy.com/topics/Evan_Roberts_(minister).

[14] "William J. Seymour Biography," website of Azusa Street, accessed August 13, 2011, http://www.azusa-street.org/WilliamJSeymour.htm.

[15] "Smith Wigglesworth," website of Cane Creek Church, Anniston, Alabama, accessed August 13, 2011, http://www.canecreekchurch.org/index.php/what—is—your—legacy/38—smith—wigglesworth.

Chapter 7—. . . And Godliness

[16] *Webster's New World Dictionary,* s.v. "godly."

[17] William E. Vine, *Vine's Expository Dictionary of Old Testament and New Testament Words,* (Nashville, TN: Thomas Nelson, 1940), WORD*search* CROSS e—book, s.v. "godliness".

[18] *Webster's New World Dictionary,* s.v. "partaker."

[19] Ibid., s.v. "barren."

[20] Adam Clarke, *A Commentary and Critical Notes,* (New York: Abingdon—Cokesbury Press, 1826), WORD*search* CROSS e—book, s.v. "The Second General Epistle of Peter".

[21] *Webster's New World Dictionary,* s.v. "unfruitful."

# BIBLIOGRAPHY

*Galaxy Quest.* Directed by Dean Parisot. Performed by Tim Allen. 1999. DVD.

Clarke, Adam. *A Commentary and Critical Notes.* New York: Abingdon—Cokesbury Press, 1826. WORD*search* CROSS e—book.

*The Matrix.* Directed by Andy Wachowski and Larry Wachowski. Performed by Laurence Fishburne and Keanu Reeves. 1999. DVD.

Ogilvie, John. *The Imperial Dictionary of the English Language: A Complete Encyclopedic Lexicon, Literary, Scientific, and Technological.* Harvard University: Blackie & Son, 1882.

Strong, James. *Strong's Talking Greek & Hebrew Dictionary.* Austin, TX: WORDsearch Corp., 2007. WORD*search* CROSS e—book.

Vine, William E. *Vine's Expository Dictionary of Old Testament and New Testament Words.* Nashville, TN: Thomas Nelson, 1940. WORD*search* CROSS e—book.

# SCRIPTURE INDEX

# WORD INDEX

# About The Author

Mike W. Ferry is the pastor of Cornerstone Christian Fellowship of Redmond, Oregon. He knew God and heard His voice at a very early age. God called Mike into ministry in 1983, and he has served in pastoral positions in churches in Texas, Pennsylvania, and Oregon. The focus of his ministry is to ignite a passion in the hearts of people to pursue a deeper relationship with God. Mike lives in Redmond, Oregon, with his wife and best friend, Patty, and their two wonderful children, Andrea and David.

# MORE INFORMATION

More copies of this book can be purchased on Amazon.com. It is also available in e-book format.

To book speaking engagements with the author, you may contact us at booking@pursuitpublishers.com. You can also find more information on the website, and a link to purchase the e-book, at http://www.PursuitPublishers.com.

There is also a website for the book, which includes excerpts from each chapter, at http://www.OfLifeAndGodliness.com.

For more information on Pastor Ferry's church, you can visit their website at http://www.ccfredmond.org.

CPSIA information can be obtained at www.ICGtesting.com
Printed in the USA
LVOW09s1412090215

426278LV00001B/61/P